Get Out of Trouble Free

As Jerry Seinfeld might say, when you start using a computer, you should get 10 "Get Out of Trouble Free" cards. Since you don't, here are some get out of trouble tips:

- Try pressing the **Esc** (Escape) key. This will usually back you out of any trouble.

- If you can't find a file and you know you didn't delete it, you probably just misplaced it. Try looking for it on a different disk or in a different directory.

- If you can't get a program to run, make sure you are typing the correct command. If the program still won't run, change to the directory that contains the program's files; then enter the command.

- If your computer freezes, wait 10 seconds. If it is still frozen, press **Ctrl+Alt+Del** to reboot it. If that doesn't work, turn it off, wait a couple of minutes, and turn it back on.

- If you have a problem with a piece of equipment, turn everything off and check the connections. You might have a loose cable.

- If you can't get your printer to print, make sure the printer has paper, is turned on, and is on-line. You might have to press an on-line button on the printer.

- If you can't get your printer to stop printing, turn off its power, wait a couple of minutes, and turn it on again.

10 Things You Should Never Do to Your Computer

Although your computer is fairly sturdy, there are some things you should never do to it:

- Don't spill anything on the keyboard.

- Don't put your computer where the sun can beat down on it.

- Don't connect anything while the power is on.

- Don't pull a disk out of the disk drive when the drive light is on.

- Don't turn off your computer until you have quit the program you were working in.

- Don't forget to save your work.

- Don't keep flipping the computer's power on and off. When you turn the computer off, wait at least a minute before turning it back on.

- Don't type the FORMAT command without specifying a drive letter A or B. For example, type **format a:** or **format b:**, not just **format**.

- Don't type **del *.*** unless you are sure you want to delete all the files in the current directory.

- Don't overestimate the intelligence of your computer.

Computer Shopping List

If you don't have a computer yet, use this card along with Chapter 18 to find the best computer at the best price. Make several copies of this card, so you have one for each dealer.

- Dealer:_____ Phone: _____

- Computer make and model:_____ Price: _____

- CPU chip (circle one):   286   386   486   Other _____
  Chip speed: _____
  Memory (RAM) installed: _____
  Expandable up to: _____   Total cost for any
                                                     extra RAM you want: _____

- RAM cache?: Yes No
  If yes, how big?: _____

- Floppy drives installed (circle one):   5.25"   3.5"   Both
  Open drive bay available for future expansion?   Yes   No   Extra cost for
                                                              another drive: _____

- Hard drive size: _____
  Transfer rate: _____
  Included?   Yes   No   Cost: _____

- Keyboard (do you like it?):   Yes   No   Extra cost for
                                                   keyboard you like: _____

- Mouse included?   Yes   No   Cost: _____

- Monitor and video card type: Monochrome EGA CGA VGA SVGA
  Included?   Yes   No   Size? _____ Inches   Cost: _____

- Printer type: _____   Cost: _____
                                                   Price of extra
                                                   ribbons or cartridges: _____

- Modem included?   Yes   No   Baud rate: _____bits per second   Cost: _____

- Number of open expansion slots: _____

- Number of parallel ports: _____

- Number of serial ports: _____

- Separate mouse port?:   Yes   No

                                                     Total Price: _____

- Software included (list software packages included and their prices):

_____ $ _____

_____ $ _____

_____ $ _____

_____ $ _____

The Complete
IDIOT'S
Guide to PCs

By Joe Kraynak

alpha
books

A Division of Prentice Hall Computer Publishing
11711 North College Avenue, Carmel, Indiana 46032 USA

To Bob Dylan, for keeping me sane.

©1993 Alpha Books

International Standard Book Number: 1-56761-168-0
Library of Congress Catalog Card Number: 92-76070

95 94 93   8 7 6 5 4 3 2

Interpretation of the printing code: the rightmost number of the first series of numbers is the year of the book's printing; the rightmost number of the second series of numbers is the number of the book's printing. For example, a printing code of 93-1 shows that the first printing of the book occurred in 1993.

Screen reproductions in this book were created by means of the program Collage Plus from Inner Media, Inc., Hollis, NH.

Printed in the United States of America

Publisher   *Marie Butler-Knight*

Associate Publisher   *Lisa A. Bucki*

Managing Editor   *Elizabeth Keaffaber*

Acquisitions Manager   *Stephen R. Poland*

Manuscript Editor   *Audra Gable*

Cover Designer   *Scott Cook*

Designer   *Amy Peppler-Adams*

Illustrations   *Steve Vanderbosch*

Indexer   *Jeanne Clark*

Production Team   *Tim Cox, Mark Enochs, Tom Loveman, Carrie Roth, Barb Webster, Kelli Widdifield*

Special thanks to C. Herbert Feltner for ensuring the technical accuracy of this book.

If for any reason you are not satisfied with this book, we will cheerfully refund your purchase price. Call this number toll-free for refund information: 1-800-428-5331.

Contents

15 "One Ringy-Dingy, Two Ringy-Dingies..." Dialing Out with Your PC — 169

16 Counting Your Chickens: Time and Money Management — 181

17 Give Me the Works: Integrated Software — 193

21 Zen and the Art of Computer Maintenance 247

IV Other Stuff You May or May Not Want to Know

22 Programs I'd Buy If You Gave Me the Money 263

Introduction

You fell for it, too. They said the computer would make your job easier, take over some of the busy work, give you more time to play tennis and bounce little Egbert on your knee. You believed them. We all did.

But now that it's time for you to start using the computer, things don't seem all that easy. The computer is about as friendly and helpful as a dead fish. And the books that came with the computer are just as bad. Sure, they have all the information you need, assuming you can find the information and translate the instructions into something that resembles English. But who has the time? You need a book that will teach you the basics: a book that tells you in plain English just what you need to know—no more, no less.

Welcome to The Complete Idiot's Guide to PCs

The Complete Idiot's Guide to PCs assumes that you are far from an idiot at the important things in life: doing your job, raising a family, buying a house, maybe even wallpapering. But some things in life have the power to confound the best of us—things like the engines in most new cars, the programming feature of a VCR, and computers. In this book I won't pack your head with high-tech fluff that will only add to the confusion. I'm not going to explain how a computer chip works, how a monitor displays pretty pictures, or how a printer prints. And I won't give you a hundred DOS commands, ninety of which you won't use. I promise.

Instead, you'll learn practical, hands-on stuff like:

- ☛ How to kick-start your computer (and restart it when all else fails).
- ☛ How to use DOS to run other programs (and avoid DOS when possible).
- ☛ What kinds of programs you can run on your computer and what you can do with them.

☛ How to get around in Microsoft Windows.

☛ How to buy a computer that's not overly obsolete.

☛ How to make your computer feel like the inferior being it is.

☛ How to get out of trouble.

You'll be surprised at how little you need to know in order to use a computer.

How Do You Use This Book?

You don't have to read this book from cover to cover (although you might miss something funny if you skip around). If you want to find out about databases, skip to the database chapter. If you want a quick lesson in using DOS, skip to the DOS chapter. Each chapter is a self-contained unit that contains the information you need to survive one aspect of the computer world.

I have used several conventions in this book to make it easier to use. For example, when you need to type something, it will appear like this:

TYPE THIS

Just type what it says. It's as simple as that.

If you want to understand more about the command you're typing in, you'll find some background information in boxes. Because this information is in boxes, you can quickly skip over the information if you want to avoid the gory details.

For real-life, timesaving ways you can use your PC, try the hands-on *Put It to Work* projects that you'll find throughout this book.

Here are some special icons used in this book that help you learn just what you need:

By the Way...
Special hints and amusing anecdotes from me.

Easy-to-understand definitions for every computer
term let you "speak like a
geek."

Skip this background fodder
(technical twaddle) unless
you're truly interested.

These notes and tips show
the easiest way to perform
some task.

There's help when things
go wrong!

Trademarks

All terms mentioned in this book that are known to be trademarks or
service marks are listed below. In addition, terms suspected of being
trademarks or service marks have been appropriately capitalized. Alpha
Books cannot attest to the accuracy of this information. Use of a term in
this book should not be regarded as affecting the validity of any trademark
or service mark.

Ami Pro, Lotus, and 1-2-3 are registered trademarks of Lotus Development
Corporation.

AutoMap is a registered trademark of NextBase Ltd.

CorelDRAW! is a registered trademark of Corel Systems Corporation.

dBASE is a trademark of the Ashton-Tate Corporation.

Part One

Getting a Grip on What You've Gotten Yourself into This Time

So, you've gotten your brand-spanking-new PC, and you have the same sinking feeling you had the day you started setting up your VCR. You opened the instructions to figure out how to get the darn thing working and realized that it was more complicated than you ever dreamed. (And programming it to tape something while you're gone might still be a dream.)

You're right to realize that it will take some time to learn how to coax your computer to do what you want it to. Enter the wrong command, and it responds with a snooty beep. Feed it the wrong disk, and it growls at you. And if you do something really unacceptable, the computer simply refuses to go on.

*The chapters in this part of **The Complete Idiot's Guide to PCs** will show you how to start getting results from your computer. You'll learn what it's made up of, how it thinks, and how you can tell it what to do. And soon, you might even look forward to spending your evenings controlling programs on disks instead of programs on VHS tapes.*

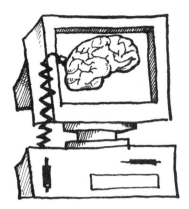

Chapter 1

Parts Is Parts: Computer Anatomy 101

In This Chapter

- The parts (hardware) that make up a computer
- Where a computer keeps its brain
- Where a computer stores information
- How the monitor shows you what's going on inside the computer
- Getting it in print
- Understanding the instructions (software) that tell your computer what to do

Welcome to *The Complete Idiot's Guide to PCs*. Although I'm the author of this book, there are still times when a computer can make me feel like an idiot. In fact, not too long ago I was a lot more at home writing information like this using a familiar and easy-to-control appliance known as a pencil. After a job change, I found myself struggling with a not-so-easy-to-control monstrosity known as a computer. I learned about computers the hard way: through trial and error. This chapter gives you a first look at a computer system, so you can learn what makes it tick with as little pain as possible.

A personal computer (or PC) is made up of a few very simple parts: a system unit, a keyboard, a mouse, a monitor (the video screen), and a printer. In this chapter, you'll learn what each part does, what it's called, and how it contributes to making your computer a computer.

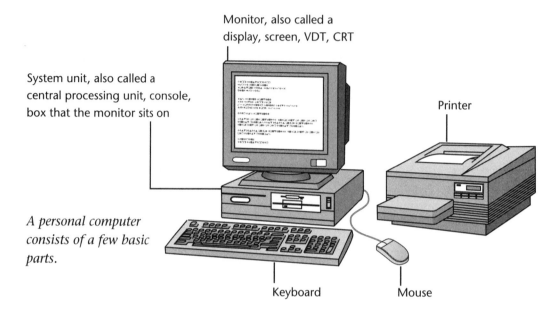

Monitor, also called a display, screen, VDT, CRT

System unit, also called a central processing unit, console, box that the monitor sits on

Printer

A personal computer consists of a few basic parts.

Keyboard   Mouse

The System Unit: Brains in a Box

Although the system unit doesn't look any more impressive than a big shoebox, it contains the following elements that enable your computer to carry out the most complex of computer operations:

Memory Chips   Memory chips store instructions and data temporarily while your computer is using them. Whenever you run a program, the program's instructions are kept in memory. Whatever you type into the computer is stored in memory so your computer can work with it. You'll learn more about memory in Chapter 4.

Central Processing Unit   The central processing unit (CPU, pronounced "sea-pea-you") is the brain of the computer. Think of the other devices connected to your system as hands and feet. The CPU sends the program instructions and information you enter to the other devices (hands and feet) to make them work. Your computer's memory chips function as holding areas for the instructions the CPU is using, much as you rely on your memory to hold facts you need to recall from time to time.

Input and Output Ports   At the back of the system unit are several outlets (ports) into which you can plug your keyboard, mouse, monitor, printer, modem, and other devices.

Floppy Disk Drives   A floppy disk drive appears as a slot on the front of the computer. Your computer may have more than one. The square plastic floppy disks you place into a drive hold program instructions and other information. The computer reads the instructions and information into memory and uses the information to do its work.

Hard Disk Drives   A hard disk drive is completely contained within your system unit and is therefore not accessible like the floppy disk drive. The hard disk itself acts as a giant floppy disk, storing hundreds of times more information. Generally, hard disk drives are not removable. You'll learn more about disk drives in Chapter 5.

Power Switch   If you have an older computer, the power switch (which is usually orange) is carefully hidden on the back, side, or front of the system unit. Chapter 3 gives more details about powering up your system.

The Keyboard: A Way to Talk to the Computer

The keyboard is made up of a lot of square keys and a wire that snakes over to the system unit.

SPEAK LIKE A GEEK

The system unit is the central part of the computer. Any devices that are attached to the system unit are considered *peripheral* (as in "peripheral vision"). Peripheral devices include the monitor, printer, keyboard, mouse, modem, and joystick. Some manufacturers consider the keyboard and monitor to be essential parts of the computer rather than peripherals.

You use most of the keys for typing numbers and letters. The additional keys give commands to the system unit. Some keys you may never use. In Chapter 5 you will find more detail on the different types and functions of keys.

Poking Around with a Mouse

A mouse is a pointing device that allows you to quickly move around on-screen and select commands by clicking on buttons rather than by pressing keys. This is what a typical mouse looks like.

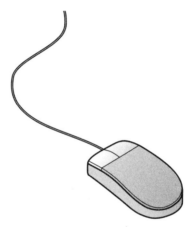

A typical mouse.

By the Way . . .

Normally, a mouse will have two buttons and no fur. Some mice have a third button in the middle, which very few programs use.

While it's not necessary to have one, a mouse can help you work faster. Most applications (programs) now work with a mouse. And for other applications—like drawing and painting programs—a mouse is required.

The Monitor: Your Computer's Windshield

The monitor is your computer's windshield. As you work, the monitor lets you see what you're doing. Whenever you run a program, the program displays a screen, menu, or *prompt* that allows you to enter a command or type text. Whatever you type appears on-screen, enabling you to see exactly which keys you are pressing.

The Printer: Getting It on Paper

The printer has all the messy parts that used to be on the typewriter: the roller, print ribbon, and the little metal arms with the letters on them (or the equivalent). The printer's job is to transform the electric burps and beeps in your computer into something that normal humans can read.

Printers range from inexpensive dot-matrix types, which print each character as a series of dots, to expensive laser printers, which operate like copy machines. In between are ink-jet printers that spray ink on the page (sounds messy, but it's not).

"Prompt" in this case means "blank stare." The computer basically looks at you and says, "Tell me something." In other words, the computer is *prompting* you or *prodding* you to enter information or a command. A prompt can look as simple as the DOS prompt, C:>, or it can appear as a message such as "Type your name and company name" in a box on-screen.

Software: Sending Your Computer to School

Before your computer can do anything useful, it needs an education; in other words, some instructions that tell it what to do. In the computer world, these instructions are called *software*.

TECHNO NERD TEACHES

The instructions that a computer follows are not in a form normal human beings can understand. The instructions are in what is called *machine language*, which consists of a series of zeros and ones. The zeros stand for Off and the ones stand for On. A program uses machine language to turn thousands of switches inside the computer on and off in a particular sequence at lightning speed, causing the computer to perform its magic.

SPEAK LIKE A GEEK

An *environment* is a setting in which you perform tasks on your computer. Microsoft Windows, for example, displays a graphical environment that lets you enter commands by selecting pictures rather than by typing commands. This makes it much easier to use your computer (assuming you know what the pictures stand for).

To illustrate how software works, imagine this. You stick a wafer in your mouth, and you automatically know how to perform brain surgery. Spit the wafer out and stick another one in your mouth. You forget all you knew about brain surgery and you are now a Certified Public Accountant.

In the case of a computer, the software comes on bite-sized disks that you can feed to the computer (using the floppy disk drive I talked about earlier). This software gives the computer all the knowledge it needs to do something useful, like calculate a budget. However, the computer's limited brain can't know everything. So when you quit the program, your computer forgets everything it learned. When you load another program, the computer learns how to do something else.

Your computer uses two basic types of software: operating system software and application software. I'll explain these next.

Operating System Software: Giving Your Computer the Basics

The operating system software provides the instructions your computer needs to live and breathe. It tells the system how to get and store information on disks, how to display information on-screen, and how to use the computer's memory and processing unit. In addition, it sets the rules by which all other programs have to play.

Two operating systems are commonly used on PCs: DOS and OS/2. Chapter 6 discusses the most popular operating system, DOS, in detail (we don't discuss OS/2). In addition, you can run Microsoft Windows, GeoWorks, or some other *environment* on top of DOS to make it easier to use. Chapter 7 provides details for working with Microsoft Windows.

Application Software: Applying the Knowledge to Useful Tasks

With an operating system, your computer has the basics, but it can't apply itself to any practical task, such as helping you write business letters or figure out whether it would pay to refinance your home.

What your computer needs is *application software*. This software consists of a set of specialized instructions your computer uses to apply itself to a useful task. This is the software (or programs) you buy to do your work (like write letters, find a phone number, or play Tetris). In Part Two of this book, you'll learn about the various types of applications and what they're good for.

The Least You Need to Know

In this chapter, you learned about the basic parts that make up a computer and the function of each part. If you don't want to pack your memory full of details, at least remember:

- ☞ The system unit contains the memory and brain power of your computer.

- ☞ The floppy disk drives, on the front of a computer, allow you to feed instructions and information on-disk into the system unit.

- ☞ A keyboard connected to the system unit allows you to type information and enter commands that tell the system unit what to do.

- ☞ A mouse is an optional device that allows you to point to and select commands and objects rather than typing commands with the keyboard.

continues

continued

☞ The monitor connects to the system unit and provides a way for you to see what's going on inside the computer and to see what you're doing.

☞ A printer transforms your work from its electronic form inside the computer to a printout on paper.

☞ Software provides your computer with the instructions it needs to operate and perform useful tasks.

☞ There are two types of software: operating system software and applications software. The operating system software gets the computer up and running. Application software provides the instructions your computer needs to perform a specific task.

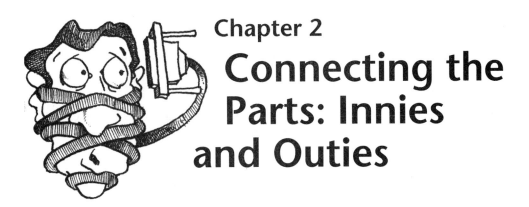

Chapter 2
Connecting the Parts: Innies and Outies

In This Chapter

- ☛ Basic rules for connecting computer equipment
- ☛ Finding a good place for your computer
- ☛ Tools and safety tips
- ☛ Unpacking all the parts
- ☛ Connecting the keyboard, mouse, monitor, and printer to the system unit
- ☛ Plugging the system unit, monitor, and printer into a power source

If your computer is set up and everything seems to be working all right, you can skip this chapter. However, if you just got the computer, and all its parts are still sitting in boxes, read this chapter to find out how easy it is to connect all the parts.

Plugs and Sockets—Pins and Holes

If you can plug in a toaster, you have all the technical knowledge you need to set up your system. Just remember one basic rule: *the pins go in the holes*. In other words, if you have a connector that has 9 pins sticking out, you have to plug it into a connector that has at least 9 holes.

Making Your Computer Feel at Home

Before you start poking pins into holes, pick a good place for your computer. This location should be:

Convenient and out of the way   Put your computer where everyone can get to it, but where no one will trip over it. Your computer should be at least as easy to get to as the TV.

Quiet   You don't want to be distracted when you are working.

Clean, cool, and dry   Dirt, heat, and moisture will damage the computer's electrical components. Don't put the computer in direct sunlight, in a damp office, or next to the clothes dryer, where lint can pour into its openings. The kitchen table is a lousy place, too.

Roomy   Plan ahead. As you get more computer equipment, software, and books, you will need room to keep everything organized. Give yourself enough room for a good sized desk and a bookcase.

Near a stable source of power   Fluctuations in power can damage your computer or the work you save. Don't plug the computer into an outlet that's on the same circuit as an appliance that draws a lot of current, such as a photocopier, space heater, or a clothes dryer.

Near a phone line   If you buy a modem for your computer, you'll have to plug the modem into an existing phone jack or install another jack. By housing the computer next to an existing phone line, you'll save yourself some work later.

Take Three Deep Breaths . . .

Before you begin, you need to gather a few tools and be aware of a few safety tips to follow to keep your system from getting damaged. The following sections provide this information.

Choose Your Weapons

You will need these tools and materials to get everything connected:

☞ A *medium sized Phillips-head screwdriver.*

☞ A *medium sized flat-head screwdriver.*

☞ A *tiny flat-head screwdriver.*

☞ A *pair of long-nosed pliers.*

☞ A *baby-food jar* (clean and empty) or a small coffee can, for storing leftovers. (It's scary, but you usually end up with four or five screws and a couple of brackets when you're done.)

Safety First

Here are some important safety tips to follow before you get started. Note that most tips keep your computer safe. As long as you don't stick your finger into a wall socket or jab a screwdriver through your hand, you'll be okay.

Instead of plugging everything into a wall outlet, get a *surge protector power strip.* A power strip contains 5 or 6 outlets, it protects your system from damaging power surges, and it enables you to turn everything on at once. Go to an electronics store and ask for it by name.

Clean your work area. You don't want to set your brand new computer in a dust bowl. Clean up before you start.

Turn on all the lights. Seeing the tiny pins and holes in the connectors is a challenge even on a sunny day. It's nearly impossible to see them in the dark.

No drinks in the work area. Drinks spill, and if your drink spills on a computer part, it may ruin the part.

Don't turn anything on till everything is connected. If you plug something in while the power is on, you might ruin the part. (I know a lady who toasted her keyboard doing this.)

Be careful with knives. If everything is still packed in boxes, try to open the boxes without cutting them. If you cut into a box, you run the risk of scratching a part or hacking through a cable.

Don't force anything. If a plug doesn't slide smoothly into an outlet, you probably have the wrong pins in the wrong holes (it's okay, it happens). Take a look at the outlet and plug again and try to match the pins to the holes.

Work close to the ground, if possible. If you drop your monitor from 6 inches off the ground, it has a fighting chance. Drop it off a table and it's history.

Unpacking the Parts

Okay, enough preliminaries. You want to see all the stuff you just shelled out two thousand bucks for, right? Dig in. Pull each part out of its box and set it on a stable surface—the floor or the desk. Take any receipts, packing slips, and other items, shove them in an envelope or bag, and stick the envelope in a safe place. You can look at the paperwork later. If books came with the computer, keep them handy—you may need them if you run into trouble.

When unpacking, keep the following tips in mind:

Don't drop anything. The parts are fragile, so take it easy. Be especially careful with the monitor; the monitor is heavier near the front (where the picture tube is), so grab it a little closer to the front.

Unpack everything. People go to school to learn how to hide things in boxes. Look for boxes inside the boxes and for crawl spaces—little compartments inside the box that can store anything from a power cord to a printer manual.

Save everything. Place all the packing material (Styrofoam, cardboard, plastic bags, and so on) in the same box it came in, and then store the boxes in the basement or attic for a couple of months (in case your computer dies a premature death or you miss something in one of the boxes).

Figuring Out Where You Want Everything to Go

Don't plug anything in until you know where you want all the parts to go. Once they're plugged in, you'll have a spaghetti bowl behind the system unit. If you then decide to move your printer or monitor, you'll be up to your ears in cables. Follow the guidelines I give next to figure out some general locations.

Set the system unit down first. Make sure the system unit can breathe; don't block the fan at the back of the unit or any of the holes on the sides or front.

While you're looking at the system unit, remove any flat cardboard pieces from the slots (the floppy disk drives) on the front of the system unit. These cardboard pieces keep the parts in the disk drives from rattling around during shipping.

Set the monitor in front of where you'll sit, screen facing you. You'll want the top of the monitor at about eye-level when you sit down (that's why many users set the monitor on the system unit).

By the Way . . .

You can raise the monitor to eye level by placing some books under it. Just make sure the monitor doesn't wobble; you don't want it to come crashing down on your desk.

If you have a mouse, set it to the left or right of where you'll sit depending on whether you are a lefty or righty. If your printer came with the rest of your computer, set it in a convenient location where you can get paper to it in a hurry.

Now, take a seat in front of your desk (or whatever you are using for a desk). Feel comfortable? Can you reach everything you'll need to reach? Think of the computer as a dashboard in a car you are test-driving. Move things around until they feel just right.

Connecting All the Parts

Now that you know where you want everything, you are ready to start connecting the parts. To figure out where to plug things in, try the following:

☞ Look for words or pictures on the back of the system unit; most receptacles are marked.

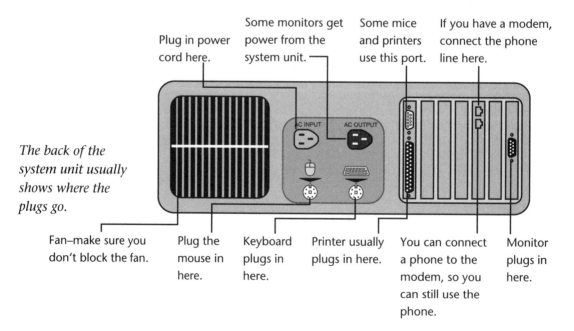

Plug in power cord here.

Some monitors get power from the system unit.

Some mice and printers use this port.

If you have a modem, connect the phone line here.

The back of the system unit usually shows where the plugs go.

Fan–make sure you don't block the fan.

Plug the mouse in here.

Keyboard plugs in here.

Printer usually plugs in here.

You can connect a phone to the modem, so you can still use the phone.

Monitor plugs in here.

☛ Try to match the plugs with their outlets. Look at the overall shape of the outlet and look to see if it has pins or holes. Count the pins and holes and make sure there are at least as many holes as there are pins.

Connecting the Monitor

The monitor has two cords: one that connects it to the system unit and one that connects it to a power supply. The following sections tell you where to connect the cords.

The receptacles at the back of the computer are called *ports* (like the ports where ships pick up and deliver cargo). In this case, the ports allow information to enter and leave the system unit.

Monitor to System Unit

Connect the monitor to the system unit first so you won't toast the monitor if the power is on. The plug that connects the monitor to the system unit has 15 pins or fewer (mine has 11). Plug it into the 15-hole socket, and then tighten the screws (if there are screws to tighten).

Monitor to Power Supply

What about the other cord? Look at the back of the computer for a power receptacle (it will look a lot like an outlet on the wall). If you find one of these outlets, *and if it matches the monitor plug*, plug the monitor into it. If not, unplug the power strip (if you got anxious and plugged it in), and then plug the power cord into the power strip.

Whenever you connect a device to one of the ports on the computer, be sure to tighten any screws or snap any clips into place. This prevents the connector from accidentally shaking loose from the port. I once had my monitor plug come loose (not completely out, but loose), and my screen turned mauve. I spent half the day figuring out the cause.

Connecting the Keyboard

The keyboard is easy to connect, once you figure out where to connect it. Some of the newer computers come with a keyboard port on the front. Other computers hide all the ports together at the back. Search for a socket that looks like the one shown here (the socket on your computer may have only five holes).

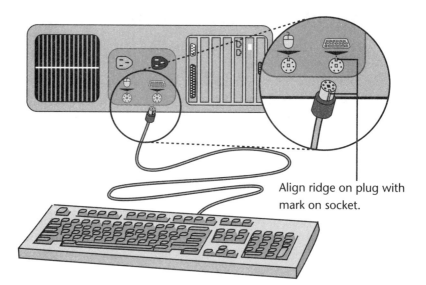

Align ridge on plug with mark on socket.

The keyboard has a port of its own.

Once you find the socket, align the pins on the plug with the holes in the socket, and slide the plug in. Most cord/socket combinations have a groove or some other marking to help you align the plug with the socket.

Don't look for a power cord; the keyboard has only one cable.

Plugging In the Mouse

The connector at the end of the mouse tail looks a lot like the connector on the keyboard cord *or* like the connector on the monitor. (In other words, depending on the mouse, the connector might look like anything.) Find a socket that matches the pins on the mouse connector: it may be labeled with a picture of a mouse or with the word "Mouse" or "COM" (COM stands for *COMmunications* port, a port commonly used for mice, printers, and modems). Find the socket and plug the mouse in.

Hooking Up the Printer

Because the printer is the most challenging computer part to set up, we saved it for last. The following sections lead you through the setup step-by-step.

Step 1: Remove the Packing Brackets

Most printers come with a sheet of paper that says "Read Me First," which tells you how to remove all the retainers and protective gear used to protect the printer during shipping. Remove all the brackets and little plastic braces and throw them in the trash.

Step 2: Where's the Cable?

The bad news is that your $500 printer probably did not come with one essential item: the cable that connects it to the system unit. The good news is that you can probably get the cable you need from an electronics store. Then again, you can probably do without the printer for a couple of days.

To figure out which cable you need, look at the printer port at the back of the computer. If it's big and has 25 holes, you'll need a 25-pin parallel printer cable. If it has 25 pins instead of holes, you'll need a serial printer cable. (Some serial ports have only 9 pins. You can buy an adapter to let you connect a 25-hole serial cable to a 9-pin serial port.) Fortunately, most computers use parallel printers, because they're faster. Make sure the cable is long enough to reach your printer, but no longer than 20 feet. At 20 feet, your printer can't hear what your system unit has to say.

TECHNO NERD TEACHES

There are two types of printers in the world: parallel and serial. Parallel printers allow the computer to send several pieces of data at the same time, using a clock to make sure the pieces arrive in the proper sequence. With serial printers, the computer must send data one piece at a time in the proper sequence, making serial printers slower than parallel printers. If given the choice of a parallel or serial printer, choose a parallel printer, unless the printer has to be more than 15 feet from your computer.

Step 3: Connect the Printer to the System Unit

Plug the cable into the printer port in the back of the computer and plug the other end into the printer. Tighten any screws to secure the cable in place. Many printers have little wire clips (instead of screws) to secure the plug in the port. Snap the clips in place.

Step 4: Connect the Printer to a Power Source

When you are done connecting the printer cable, plug the power cord into the power strip.

Connecting Other Equipment

If you have any parts left over that have cables, you'll need to plug them in somewhere. Just try to find a socket that matches the plug, and go for it.

If you have a circuit board that needs to be installed (for example, an internal modem or a card for a joystick), skip ahead to Chapter 20, where we show you the basics of installing additional parts.

Taking Care of Warranties and Registration Cards

Remember all the paperwork you shoved in the envelope or bag? Get it out and look for any cards or paper that have "Warranty" or "Registration" or "Read Me First" printed on them. Fill out any cards and mail them in. That way, if your system dies in its first year or so of life, you can get it fixed for free.

By the Way . . .

Many computers come with free software that you can get by mailing in a card. Using this card trick, I got three free programs worth about 500 bucks. Keep an eye out for these cards.

If your computer came with any software in boxes, open the boxes, look for the registration cards, fill them out, and mail them in. Why fill out all this garbage? For several reasons:

☞ You'll be able to get technical support of some sort if your software is registered.

☞ If a company decides to upgrade its equipment or programs, the company will notify registered users and usually let them buy the upgrade at a reduced price.

☞ You'll have a secure feeling, knowing that if the pirate police raid your house or business, you'll have only bona fide, registered, paid-for versions of your software.

Setting Up DOS

In all likelihood, you won't have to set up DOS. Most computer manufacturers or dealers install DOS on the computer's hard disk in order to test the computer before shipping it. To find out if DOS is installed, skip ahead to the next chapter about turning on your computer. If you turn it on and a message appears on the screen telling you that the computer cannot find a system disk, DOS is not installed.

If DOS is not installed, you have a couple of options, as explained in the next few sections.

Get the Sales Person to Install DOS for You

If you bought the computer from the local neighborhood computer store, get the guy who sold it to you to install DOS for you.

Run the DOS Setup Program

Look for the DOS Setup disk (it might be labeled Setup or Install or Disk 1). When you find the disk, perform the following steps:

Installing a mouse and other software. If you have a mouse or other software, it may already be installed, as well. If it is not, you'll learn how to install software in Chapter 8.

With your computer off, insert the disk into the top or left floppy drive on the front of the computer (refer to Chapter 5 for details on floppy disks). Close the drive door.

Turn on your computer. A message will appear on-screen telling you what to do. Follow the on-screen instructions to install DOS. The setup program will ask you a lot of questions. If you don't know an answer, just press **Enter**.

The Least You Need to Know

In this chapter, you learned all the details about connecting the various parts that make up your computer. This list provides the bare essentials:

- ☞ Before you start, make sure all equipment is unplugged and turned off.

- ☞ Pictures or words on the back of the computer usually tell you where to connect each device.

- ☞ The connector for the monitor has up to 15 pins. Plug the monitor into the 15-hole outlet; then plug the monitor into a power source.

- ☞ The keyboard connector has 5 or 6 pins. Plug it into the keyboard port at the back or front of the computer.

- ☞ If you have a mouse, plug it into the mouse port or one of the COM ports (usually COM1).

- ☞ If you have a parallel printer, connect it to the 25-hole female port at the back of the computer. This port should be labeled Parallel, Printer, or LPT1. Then plug the printer into a power source.

- ☞ If you have a serial printer, connect it to the 25-pin male COM port; then plug the printer into a power source.

Chapter 3
Turning On the Juice

In This Chapter

- How to turn on the parts of your computer
- Turning everything on with the power strip
- What it means to "boot" your computer
- Cold booting and warm booting
- Turning off your computer

In order for your computer to become a living, thinking being, you have to turn it on. In this chapter, I will tell you which switches you need to flip and in what order (even though it really doesn't matter). I'll tell you how most computers respond to the rude awakening known as "the boot" (or "das boot" in German). And you'll learn how to turn the computer off. Don't worry—nothing you do in this chapter will hurt your computer.

Firing Up the Power Strip

If you have everything plugged into a power strip, you have to turn on the power strip first to get electricity to the other plugs. Otherwise, when you turn on your monitor and system unit, nothing will happen.

First, make sure the power strip is plugged in. Flip the switch on the power strip. Some power strips have a small light that winks at you to let you know the strip is on.

Monitor First

Although you can turn on a monitor at any time, waiting till later is like driving your car before you scrape the snow off the windshield. As long as the monitor is off, you won't be able to see what's going on.

OOPS!

Powering up your monitor and printer before you turn on the system unit can prolong your computer's life. When the system unit is on, powering up another device sends a power surge to the system unit. This kind of power surge can eventually fry delicate parts of the system unit. So, turn on your monitor and printer first.

To turn on your monitor, first find the power switch. Try the back of the monitor, the side, or the last place you'd ever look—right on the front of the monitor.

Flip the switch or press the power button. If there is a I and an O on the switch, just remember that I means "on," and O means "off." You'll hear a high-pitched whistle like the one you hear when you turn on your TV. Don't worry if the screen is still blank. It remains blank until you turn on the system unit.

What About the Printer?

If you want to use the printer, go ahead and turn it on. If you're not going to use it right now, you can leave it off. The printer doesn't need to be on for you to use the rest of the computer, and you have bigger fish to fry. When you need the printer, use these steps to turn it on:

☞ Find the power switch or button.

☞ Flip the switch or press the button.

☞ Look for a button labeled "Online" or "On Line." If you find it, make sure the light next to it is lit (not flashing). If it's flashing or off, you probably need to load paper in the printer. If you're not out of paper, pressing the button will probably turn the light on.

Giving Your Computer a Good, Swift Kick in the Pants

Your computer is a heavy sleeper; to wake it, you have to "boot" it. You have to turn your computer on with the operating system instructions (DOS) in place. That is, DOS must be installed on the computer's hard disk, or the DOS startup disk must be in the first floppy disk drive.

By the Way . . .

The term boot has nothing to do with kicking your computer. Powering up pulls DOS's instructions into your computer's memory so it can get to work. This is much like "pulling yourself up by your own bootstraps" so you can face another day at the office.

How do you know if DOS is installed on your computer's hard disk? Turn on your computer, as explained in the next section. Watch the screen and listen to the computer. When the computer quiets down and the screen stops changing, look at the screen. If DOS is not installed, a message will appear on-screen telling you that a non-system disk is in the drive. Later in this chapter, you'll learn what to do if DOS is not installed.

Booting Your Computer from the Hard Disk

Booting your computer from the hard disk drive basically consists of flipping the system unit's power switch to the On position.

Before you flip the switch, however, you need to remove any disks from the floppy disk drives (the slots on the front of the computer). You may have to flip a lever, lift a door, or press an eject button below the disk drive. Then, pull the disk out.

Then find the system unit power switch or button. It's there somewhere. Try the back of the system unit, the side, or the front. Flip the switch or press the power button. Text will appear on-screen, the disk drive activity lights will turn on and off, and you will hear beeps and grinding sounds. This is all normal.

What happens if you leave a floppy disk in the drive? When you turn on the computer, you'll hear some grinding as your computer tries to read DOS off the floppy disk. Then, a message will appear on the monitor, telling you that there is a non-system disk in the drive. No biggy—remove the disk from the floppy disk drive and press **Ctrl+Alt+Delete**. The computer will now look to the hard disk to find DOS.

Booting Your Computer from a Floppy Disk

Newer computers have hard disks, so you may never need to boot your computer from a floppy disk. However, if you come across an ancient computer or if you cannot boot from the hard disk drive (for whatever reason), here's what to do:

Make sure the DOS program disk you're using is write protected. Write protecting prevents your computer from making any changes to the data on the disk. If your disk is a 5 1/4-inch disk with a notch in the right side, make sure there's tape folded over it (most boxes of 5 1/4-inch disks come with sticky tabs for this purpose). For a 3 1/2-inch disk, slide the corner tab until you can see through a little "window" in the disk. If you need to change files on a write-protected disk, unprotect it first.

☞ Hold the DOS program disk (Disk 1) by its label (label facing up) and insert the opposite end into the floppy disk drive (the top or left slot on the front of the computer). If the floppy drive has a door, close it.

☞ Turn on the power to your computer. The computer starts and loads DOS into memory.

The Computer Starts to Wake Up

As your computer boots, you'll see some text appear on-screen as the computer goes through its internal checks. The disk drive lights will go on and off, and you will hear the floppy disk drives grind. The computer is basically making sure all its parts are still in working order.

Does Anybody Really Know What Time It Is?

Most computers have an internal, battery-operated clock that keeps track of the current date and time. When you boot your computer, DOS may ask you to enter today's date and the current time. Here's what you do:

☞ Type the date in the requested format. For example, if DOS prompts you to type the date in the format MM-DD-YY (Month-Day-Year), type something like **04-25-93**. Press **Enter**.

☞ Type the time in the requested format. For example, if DOS prompts you to type the time in the format HH:MM:SS (Hour:Minute:Second), type something like **08:33:05**. Press **Enter**.

Every computer comes with a built-in set of instructions that tell it how to get started and where to look for DOS. One of the first things the startup instructions do is perform a Power-On Self-Test (POST for short). If the test reveals that any component is not working properly, the computer displays an error message on-screen giving a general indication of which component is causing problems.

DOS, Are You There?

When the system quiets down, you should see a *prompt* on-screen that looks something like this: **C:\>** or **C:>** or **C>** or **A>**. If you don't see the prompt, don't panic. Several things may be going on:

Blank screen. If your screen is still blank, make sure the monitor is turned on. If it's on, the brightness knob may be turned way down. Try turning the brightness up.

Non-system disk or disk error. If you see a message telling you that there is a non-system disk in the drive, try the following solutions:

If you left a disk in the floppy drive by mistake, remove the disk and press any key on the keyboard.

If that doesn't work, your computer may not have a hard disk drive. You will have to boot the computer from a floppy disk.

If your computer has a hard disk drive, DOS may not be installed on it. Go back to Chapter 2 to learn how to install DOS.

A screen with small pictures appears. If you see a pretty screen with lots of pictures, the dealer probably set up Microsoft Windows or some other graphic program to run automatically on your computer. Skip ahead to Chapter 8 *"Taking the Pain Out of Microsoft Windows"* to determine what to do.

A menu program appears on-screen. If you see a list of choices, the dealer probably set up a menu program to make your computer easier to use.

What's Wrong with This Picture?

Say that you turn on your computer and the following message appears on-screen: **Keyboard failure**. You look at the keyboard and realize that it is not connected to the system unit, so you plug it in.

Answer: You should never connect anything to the system unit while it is on. Turn the system unit off, connect the keyboard, and then reboot the computer.

Turning Everything On at the Power Strip

You've seen it before. Some guy walks up to his computer, flips a single switch, and all the lights come on—monitor, system unit, printer, the works. How'd he do that? The answer is the power strip. The secret is that once everything is on, you turn it off and on from the power strip. This saves wear-and-tear on switches and buttons and gets everything up and running in a hurry.

> **By the Way . . .**
>
> If you try to turn everything on from the power strip and it doesn't work, don't do it anymore. It's not for everybody, and it may not be the best idea for your computer system.

Cold Boots, Warm Boots, and the Reset Button

When you turn on your computer, electricity flows through the system like blood through veins, warming your computer's innards. Then, the computer reads its startup instructions and starts thinking. This is called a *cold boot* because your computer has to warm its chips before it can start doing anything else.

TECHNO NERD TEACHES

Ideally, you should cold boot your computer only once each day—when you first turn it on. If you keep warming and cooling its chips all day, you place added stress on the chips and other parts and may cause them to wear out early.

Warm Booting: Rebooting Your Computer

During the day, your computer may lock up, refusing to do any more work. You press **Esc**, click the mouse everywhere, press the **F1** key, press all the other keys, and it gives you the same blank stare.

When this happens, you will be tempted to turn the computer off and then on. Resist the temptation. Try to *warm boot* the computer first. To warm boot the computer, hold down the **Ctrl** key and the **Alt** key while pressing the **Del** key. This key combination (Ctrl+Alt+Del) is commonly referred to as the "three-key salute." Warm booting is preferred to cold booting because it doesn't stress out your computer.

Reboot your computer only as a last resort. If you are working on a project and you have to reboot, anything you did since the last time you saved your work will be lost.

The Reset Button

Sometimes the Ctrl+Alt+Del key combination does not work. You press the combination, and nothing happens. What next? If your computer has a **Reset** button, try pressing it to reboot your computer. Like Ctrl+Alt+Del, the Reset button reboots your computer without turning the power off and on.

Cold Booting: The Last Resort

If a warm boot does not work and your computer does not have a Reset button, you will have to cold boot your computer. To cold boot your computer, start by flipping the system unit power switch to the Off position.

Wait 15 to 30 seconds for the system to come to a complete rest and to allow the system to clear everything from memory. Listen to your computer carefully, and you'll be able to hear it "power down" for a few seconds. After the sound of powering down ends, flip the system unit power switch to the On position.

Turning Everything Off

Turning your computer off is more complicated than turning it on. The reason for this is that you have probably done other things with your computer since starting it. To turn off the computer, you have to first back out of whatever you were doing. Then take the following steps to turn off your computer.

- ☞ **Save anything you've been doing on a disk.** As you'll see in the next chapter, your work is stored as electronic blips in your computer's memory. If you turn off the juice without saving your work on a disk, your computer forgets everything in its electronic memory.

- ☞ **Quit any programs you are currently using.** When you close a program, the program makes sure you've saved all your work to disk, and then it shuts itself down properly. If you turn off the power without quitting your programs, you might lose your work.

☞ **Put your floppy disks away.** Floppy disks can get damaged if you leave them in the disk drives. Remove the floppy disks from the disk drives and put them away. Make sure that the floppy drive light goes off before you pull out the disk.

☞ **Turn off your computer.** Flip the power button on the power strip, or flip each switch or button on the individual computer parts.

The Least You Need to Know

In this chapter, you learned everything you need to know about turning a computer on and off. You also learned a lot of things you don't need to know. So, here's what you absolutely need to know:

☞ Before you turn anything on, make sure everything is plugged in and the power strip (if you have one) is turned on.

☞ Turn on the monitor and printer first, and then the system unit.

☞ If DOS is installed on your computer's hard disk, the computer will automatically boot and be ready to run other programs.

☞ If you turn on your computer and it displays the message **Non-system disk or disk error**, you probably left a disk in the floppy disk drive by mistake. Remove the disk and press any key on the keyboard.

☞ If you have a computer without a hard disk drive, you must boot from a floppy disk.

☞ If your computer locks up, try to warm boot it by pressing **Ctrl+Alt+Del**.

☞ Before you turn off your computer, save any work you've done and quit any programs you were using.

Chapter 4
"Hey, What's Going On in There?"

In This Chapter

- ☞ What happens when you start your computer
- ☞ ROM (read-only memory): How your computer uses it
- ☞ RAM (random-access memory): What RAM is and what RAM does
- ☞ Where DOS comes in
- ☞ Why your computer needs disks
- ☞ What happens when you run a program
- ☞ What happens when you type information

You don't really need to know the anatomy and physiology of your car in order to drive it. Nor do you need to know much about the innards of a computer in order to type a letter. However, for the technically curious, this chapter will tell you a little bit about what's going on under the hood of your PC. If you're not curious, put your foot on the accelerator and floor it! (I'll catch up to you in Chapter 5.)

Without a BIOS, Your PC Is Comatose

When you start your car, it pretty much knows what to do. It sends some gas/air mixture and some sparks to the cylinders and starts a series of controlled explosions that sets everything in motion. Your PC does much the same thing without the gas. It reads some startup instructions off a set of memory chips and then it looks for an operating system, usually DOS.

Where Does It Start?

The start-up instructions are called the BIOS (pronounced "BUY-ose") or System BIOS (BIOS stands for *basic input-output system*). The BIOS is stored on a ROM chip that's connected to the CPU. ROM (which rhymes with "mom") stands for *read-only memory*; your computer can read the BIOS off the chip but cannot change it.

BIOS: Your Friendly Computer Traffic Controller

The BIOS lets your computer's CPU control traffic between the various elements that make up the computer, including disk drives, the printer, the ports, and the monitor. When you turn on your computer, it first reads these instructions, performs a series of internal tests, and then looks for another chip, CMOS.

By the Way . . . BIOS Sightings

Your BIOS is about as reclusive as the abominable snowman. To find out what kind of BIOS you have, watch the monitor when you first turn on your computer, and you might get a glimpse of it; it should be the first text you see on-screen. Look for Phoenix, Award, or AMI (AM-Mee). These are the manufacturers who design the BIOS's used on 90% of all PCs.

A Check-Check Here and a Check-Check There . . .

All the grunts, grinds, and beeps your computer emits when you turn it on are a sign that your computer is checking itself out. Watch the screen, and you will see the computer tallying the amount of memory it has. See the disk drive lights come on? Hear the drives grind? That's the computer making sure the disk drives are still there.

Once the BIOS is done checking the various parts of the computer, it compares its findings with information stored in the CMOS, as explained in the following section.

More than Just an Acronym: Battery-Powered Memory Called CMOS

CMOS, pronounced "sea-moss," is a battery-powered device that stores important information, including the date and time, the number of disk drives the computer has, the type of monitor it's using, and how much memory is installed.

When you start your computer, the BIOS compares the results of its internal checks with the information stored in the CMOS. Assuming everything checks out, the computer reads the information from the CMOS to determine the date and time and other information about the computer.

CMOS stands for Complementary Metal-Oxide Semiconductor. When most people talk about their CMOS, however, they are talking about the information stored on the CMOS, not about the CMOS itself. So if you hear someone say, "My CMOS got wiped out, and now I have no C drive," the person probably means that the information about the hard drive was deleted from the CMOS and now the computer does not know it has a drive C.

When the computer is done reading the CMOS information, it checks drive A to see if the DOS startup disk is in the floppy drive. Assuming there is no disk in drive A, the computer looks for DOS on the hard disk.

Taking Orders from the Boss, DOS

Okay, so far, your computer has read BIOS and CMOS, and checked itself out. What next? Assuming the DOS files are on the computer's hard disk or on a disk that is in the computer's floppy drive, the computer reads DOS and stores its instructions in RAM. (RAM, which rhymes with "bam," is your computer's temporary memory.) A *prompt* (a message telling you that your computer is waiting for a command or information) appears on-screen. This is DOS—the not-so-friendly operating system that runs your computer.

DOS, the poker face of the computer industry.

By the Way . . .

I'll save my DOS insults for Chapter 6. In this chapter, I just want to give you some idea of what's going on inside your computer as you start it and work with other programs. You also may want to read this information again if your computer is giving you problems when it boots.

So Why Does DOS Need to Be in RAM, Anyway?

So, your computer has read the DOS instructions from disk and stored them in RAM. Why? The reason is that it takes awhile for your computer to read information off a disk, whereas the computer can get information from RAM almost instantaneously. By keeping DOS in RAM, the computer has DOS at its fingertips.

The Disk-RAM Connection

To understand how your computer gets and stores information, think of a disk as a book, and think of RAM as your own memory. When you need information that is not in your memory, you must read a book or article to get the information you need. The information is then stored in your memory, where you can work with it: interpret it, react to it, compare it to other things you've read, and even forget it.

Your computer works the same way. It reads information or instructions off of disks and stores the information in RAM, where it can get at the information more quickly.

RAM: Short-Term Parking

RAM is made up of several components called *chips* that store information electronically. The information remains in RAM only as long as the electricity is flowing. If you open a document in RAM and then turn off the computer or experience a power outage, RAM "forgets" the document. Whatever you saved on disk is safe, but any changes you made to the document are lost.

What is a chip? A single chip contains over a million microscopic switches that can be turned on and off in various combinations to represent information. To understand how a memory chip works, keep in mind that a computer uses binary numbers to store information. A binary number consists of a series of ones and zeros. (One stands for a switch that's On, and zero stands for a switch that's Off.) For example, the letter A is represented as 01000001.

Disks: Long-Term Parking

Disks (floppy and hard) store information permanently (or at least until you erase it). Think of a disk as a cassette tape. Just as you can store sounds on a cassette tape, you can store data on a disk and later "play back" the data on your computer.

Just as with cassette tapes, you can buy disks that already have information on them. For example, you can buy disks that have the program instructions for *WordPerfect* or for the computer game *Where in the World is Carmen Sandiego?*. You can then "play" the disk on your computer and use the program to do your work or avoid work entirely.

Application Programs: Doing the Grunt Work for DOS

Remember, DOS is the boss; it doesn't do any real work. It just stays in the background and makes sure everything else does what it's supposed to do. Once DOS is running, you can run specialized programs, such as word-processing, spreadsheet, or database programs. These programs are called *applications*, because they allow you to "apply" the computer to some useful task, such as writing a letter, balancing your budget, or playing a game.

When you run an application, your computer reads the program's instructions from disk and stores them in RAM, just as it did with DOS. You can then use the program to do your work or play a game. When you quit the program, it is removed from RAM. You'll learn how to run programs in Chapters 6 and 7.

Saving Your Data from RAM to Disk

Once DOS and your application are running, you can use your application to type a letter, enter numbers, create a picture, or perform some other task, depending on the application.

As you work, keep in mind that whatever you create is stored electronically in RAM. If you turn off your computer (or if the power goes out) before you save your work, it will be lost forever.

Chapter 6 explains more of the nitty-gritty details about files. You use a different command or keystroke to save files in different applications; however, many newer applications simply offer a command called "Save," generally located on a menu called "File."

To prevent your work from being forgotten, you must save it to a disk—a permanent, magnetic storage device. Whenever you save your work, it is saved in a special *file* which you must name. During the save operation, the computer writes the electronic data from RAM to the magnetic disk. The computer uses the file name to track where the data is stored.

Some programs offer a feature called *autosave*, which means that you can tell the program to save your work automatically every few minutes or so.

Getting Your Work from Disk to RAM

Your application may use a different name for opening a file, such as "getting" or "retrieving" a file.

Once your work is saved on disk, you can read your work from disk and continue working on it later. However, in order to open the file you saved, you must first run the application in which you created the file. When you open the file, your work will appear on-screen, ready for your changes.

The Least You Need to Know

Now that you've read all the details, here is a brief overview of what happens when you start and use your computer:

- ☞ Your computer reads the BIOS off a set of ROM chips. The BIOS performs two basic operations: it performs a series of internal tests, and it looks for an operating system.

- ☞ After testing the computer's components, the BIOS checks its findings against the information in CMOS.

- ☞ Assuming the computer's components are functioning properly, the BIOS looks for the operating system—DOS.

- ☞ The computer loads DOS from disk into RAM.

- ☞ You can now load other programs into RAM and use those programs to perform specific tasks.

- ☞ As you type, draw, or perform some other task, your work is stored in RAM.

- ☞ To prevent your work from getting lost when you turn off the power, you must save your work from RAM to disk.

- ☞ To work on a file that you have saved to disk, you must first run the program in which you created the file and then open the file.

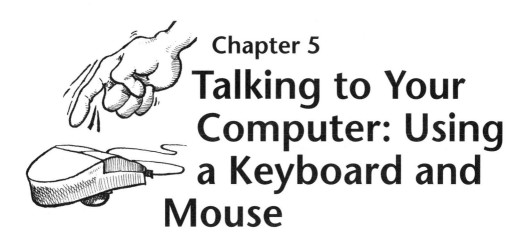

Chapter 5

Talking to Your Computer: Using a Keyboard and Mouse

In This Chapter

- Using a keyboard to talk to your computer
- The special and not-so-special keys on a keyboard
- How to use a mouse to communicate with a program
- Problems that mouse users commonly have when first learning to use a mouse

Someday, we will all be barking orders at voice-activated computers. Instead of typing a report or story, we will dictate it and have the computer worry about the grammar and spelling. Instead of typing in a list of numbers, we will read them to the computer. We will be able to do all our computing while sitting in a nice, steamy jacuzzi. Ahhh, technology! Until then, however, we must rely on a couple of more primitive gadgets: the keyboard and the mouse.

Pecking Away at the Keyboard

The keyboard owes its success to its simplicity. It contains the letter and number keys you need for entering data, function keys for entering commands, and arrow keys for moving around on-screen. Whether you are a touch typist or a master of the hunt-and-peck technique, you will find that the keyboard gives you complete control over your computer.

Keys, Keys, and More Keys

Although the locations of keys on your keyboard may vary, all PC keyboards contain some standard keys:

Alphanumeric keys   *Alphanumeric* is a fancy term for "letters and numbers." This area of the keyboard also includes a Shift key (for uppercase letters), an Enter (or Return) key, a Spacebar, a Tab key, and a Backspace key.

Function keys   The function keys are the 10 or 12 F keys ("eff" keys) at the top or left side of the keyboard. These keys are numbered F1, F2, F3, and so on. You'll use them for entering commands. Which commands? That depends on the program.

Arrow keys   Also known as cursor-movement keys, the arrow keys move the cursor (the blinking line or box) around on-screen.

Numeric keypad   The numeric keypad consists of a group of number keys positioned like the keys on an adding machine. This keypad includes a Num Lock key. With Num Lock turned off, you use the numeric keypad to move around on-screen. With Num Lock turned on, you use the keypad to type numbers.

Ctrl and Alt keys   The Ctrl (Control) and Alt (Alternative) keys make the other keys on the keyboard act differently from the way they normally act. For example, if you press the F1 key by itself, the computer may display a help screen, but if you hold down the Ctrl key while pressing F1 (Ctrl+F1, in computer lingo), the computer will carry out an entirely different command.

Esc key   You can use the Esc (Escape) key in most programs to back out of or quit whatever you are currently doing. (In WordPerfect, however, you use the F1 key to back out of things.)

Stupid Keyboard Tricks

To get a feel for the keyboard, try typing some text at the DOS prompt. First, type **cd \dos** and press **Enter**. This changes to the DOS directory (the place where most DOS files are stored). Now, type **dir** and press **Enter**. A list of files flies past the screen.

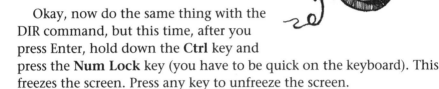

Okay, now do the same thing with the DIR command, but this time, after you press Enter, hold down the **Ctrl** key and press the **Num Lock** key (you have to be quick on the keyboard). This freezes the screen. Press any key to unfreeze the screen.

One last trick. Press the **F3** key. Voilà! The DIR command reappears at the DOS prompt. Press **Backspace** three times to delete the DIR command. Now press the **F1** key three times. This places the DIR command at the DOS prompt one character at a time.

Scurrying About with a Mouse

Although the keyboard allows you to move around on the screen and enter commands and text, it's fairly stiff as far as control mechanisms go. Sometimes, you need a more fluid device, something that allows you to fly from one corner of the screen to another, non-stop. You need a mouse.

The Mouse and Its Pointer

If you have a mouse and a program that *supports* (allows you to use) a mouse, a mouse pointer will appear on-screen when you start the program. The appearance of the pointer varies depending on the program. Sometimes it looks like a tall rectangle. Other times, it looks like an arrow. It may even appear as a cross hair pointer (like what you see when you look through a rifle sight).

> **By the Way . . .**
>
> If you start a program and you don't see the mouse pointer, roll the mouse around on the desktop until the pointer comes into view.

Mouse Poking Techniques

The neat thing about a mouse is that you really don't have to know what you're doing in a program in order to use the program. You just poke around with the mouse until you find something useful. However, you do have to know how to poke around.

To poke around with the mouse, you roll the mouse on the desktop until the mouse pointer is over the item you want. This is called *pointing*, and it really doesn't do anything.

Once you have pointed to something, you can select it by *clicking* (pressing and releasing) the mouse button. (You'll hear the mouse button click.) You'll usually use the left mouse button. Programs reserve the right mouse button for cancelling a selection or for other special actions.

Once you've mastered the click, you'll want to tackle the more powerful *double-click*. This consists of pointing to an object on-screen and then pressing and releasing the left mouse button twice quickly without moving the mouse. You usually double-click to give a command, select a file, or start a program.

The last move in the mousecapades' repertoire is the *drag*. Dragging consists of holding down the mouse button while moving the mouse. You usually drag to select letters or words, move something on-screen, or draw a line or shape.

Getting Along with Your Mouse

Mice are moody little varmints, and you have to get used to their moods. If you're just starting out with a mouse, you are likely to make the same mistakes we have all made. Trouble is, when you are making the mistakes, it's hard to tell what you're doing wrong. Here are some pointers.

First, hold still when clicking. If you move when you're clicking, you might just move the mouse pointer off the item you wanted to select. For example, you might choose Delete instead of Copy.

Next, remember to click to select, double-click to enter. If you click on something, it is selected, but nothing will happen. If you want something to happen, click-click. Also, when double-clicking, do it quickly. Two clicks is not a double-click. If you click twice slowly, you will select an item twice.

Finally, keep an eye on the other cursor. When you are working with text (letters and words), you have two cursors: the mouse pointer and a text cursor (a vertical or horizontal bar). When you start typing, text is entered at the text cursor, not at the mouse pointer. To move the text cursor, you must use the mouse to click where you want the text cursor placed.

Making Your Mouse Behave

Most programs allow you to change the mouse settings to make the mouse behave the way you want it to. If your mouse seems slow, for example, you can increase the speed at which the pointer moves across the screen.

Cursor or Insertion Point?   Both a cursor and an insertion point show you where the text you type will appear. A cursor is a horizontal line or a flashing box that appears below or on top of characters. The insertion point is a vertical line that appears between characters. Although they are basically the same, in DOS programs you see the cursor, and in Windows programs you see both the insertion point and the cursor.

You can also adjust the double-click interval if your trigger finger is getting slow. By increasing the double-click interval, you can click twice a little more slowly and still have a double-click.

You can also "flip" the left and right mouse buttons if you are left-handed. You don't actually flip the buttons—you just tell the program to treat the left mouse button as the right button and vice versa.

The Least You Need to Know

Because the keyboard and mouse give you a way to talk to your computer, it is important that you know the basic keyboard and mouse moves:

- ☞ With a keyboard, use the function keys (F1, F2, F3, and so on) to enter commands. The commands vary from program to program.

- ☞ The arrow keys allow you to move around on-screen.

- ☞ The main portion of the keyboard contains numbers and letters that allow you to enter information into the computer.

- ☞ A mouse allows you to select items on-screen.

- ☞ To select an item with the mouse, point to the item on-screen, and then press and release the left mouse button.

- ☞ If you need to drag something on-screen, move the mouse pointer over the item, and then hold down the left mouse button while moving the mouse.

Chapter 6

Feeding Your Computer: Disks, Files, and Other Munchies

In This Chapter

- ☛ Disk drives and the letters that identify them
- ☛ What a floppy disk drive is and why you need at least one
- ☛ How to handle a floppy disk without damaging the disk or the information it contains
- ☛ How to insert and remove floppy disks from their drives
- ☛ How to prepare disks to store information
- ☛ How to organize files on a hard disk by using directories

One of the most important jobs you have as a computer user is to keep your computer fed. Computers eat bite-size, cracker-shaped things called *disks*. Well, they don't actually eat the disks. They just lick information off the disks, sort of like licking dip off chips. The computer reads the information off the disks and stores it in memory where the computer can use the information.

So, if it's that simple, why have an entire chapter devoted to it? Because it's not that simple. Computers make everything complicated.

Disk Drives: As Easy As A B C

Most computers have three disk drives, as shown here. DOS refers to the drives as A, B, and C.

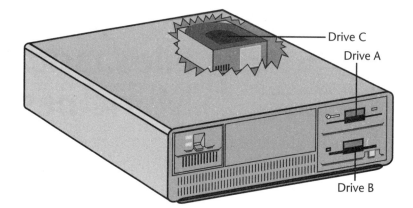

Drive C
Drive A
Drive B

DOS refers to disk drives using letters from the alphabet.

A disk is a circular piece of plastic that's covered with microscopic magnetic particles. A disk drive inside the computer can "read" the charges of the magnetic particles and convert them to electrical charges that are stored in the computer's memory. The drive can also write information from RAM to the disk by changing the charge of the magnetic particles. Disks come in two basic types, hard and floppy. Floppy disks are the kind you stick in the slots on the front of the computer. Hard disks are typically sealed inside the computer.

The Floppy Disk Drives: A and B

The two drives on the front of the computer are the *floppy disk drives* (the drive's not floppy, the disk is). The top drive is usually drive A. The bottom drive is usually drive B. If your computer has only one floppy disk drive, it is drive A, and there is no drive B.

The Hard Disk Drive: C

The drive shown inside the computer is the *internal hard disk drive*, usually called drive C. Some computers have an *external* hard drive, which sits outside of the computer and is connected to the system unit by a cable (it's still drive C).

Take a Tour of Your Drives

If you're sitting at your computer, try changing to a drive. Type **a:** (that's the drive letter followed by a colon) and press **Enter**. If you hear a grinding sound and see the following message on-screen

> **Not ready reading drive A**
> **Abort, Retry, Fail?**

there's no disk in drive A. Stick a disk in the drive, close the drive door, and press **R** for Retry. The DOS prompt will now appear something like this: **A:>**. You have successfully changed to drive A.

To change back to drive C, type **c:** and press **Enter**. Do you have a drive D? Type **d:** and press **Enter**. If you see a message that says

> **Invalid drive specification**

your computer has no drive D (most computers nowadays only go up to C). If you do have a drive D, you might have an E, F, and G. Try changing to those drives.

SPEAK LIKE A GEEK

A hard disk drive can be divided (or *partitioned*) into one or more drives, which DOS refers to as drive C, drive D, drive E, and so on. (Don't be fooled; it's still one disk drive.) The actual hard disk drive is called the *physical* drive; each partition is called a *logical* drive.

Serving Information to the Computer on Floppy Disks

Think of a floppy disk as a serving tray. Whenever you want to get information into the computer, you must deliver the information on a floppy disk. Likewise, if there is something in your computer that you want to store for safekeeping or share with another user, you can copy the information from the computer to a floppy disk. You can then remove the floppy disk and stick it in a drawer or give it to a friend.

Two Sizes Fit All

Two characteristics describe floppy disks: *size* and *capacity*. Size you can measure with a ruler. The size tells you which floppy drive the disk will fit in. You can get 3 1/2-inch disks or 5 1/4-inch disks, as shown here.

5 1/4" disk

3 1/2" disk

Floppy disks come in two sizes.

Capacity: How Much Will It Hold?

To understand density, think of a disk covered with magnetic dust. Each particle of dust stores one piece of data. No matter how large or small the particle, it still stores only one piece of data. With low-density disks, the particles are large, so the disk can hold fewer particles (less data). With high-density disks, the particles are small, so more particles can be packed into less space, and the disk can store more data.

Capacity refers to the amount of information the disk can hold; it's sort of like pints, quarts, and gallons. Capacity is measured in *kilobytes (K)* and *megabytes (MB)*. Each *byte* consists of 8 *bits* and is used to store a single character—A, B, C, 1, 2, 3, and so on. (For example, 01000001 is a byte that represents an uppercase A; each 1 or 0 is a bit.) A kilobyte is 1,024 bytes—1,024 characters. A megabyte is a little over a million bytes. Grababyte means go get lunch.

One Side or Two?

A disk's capacity depends on whether it stores information on one side (single-sided) or both sides (double-sided) of the disk and on how much information it lets you cram into a given amount of space (the disk's *density*).

The Bottom Line: Types of Floppy Disks

Table 6.1 shows the four basic types of floppy disks and how much information each type can hold.

Table 6.1   Four Basic Types of Floppy Disks

Disk Size	Disk Type	Disk Capacity
5-1/4"	Double-sided Double-density (DS/DD)	360K
5-1/4"	Double-sided High-density (DS/HD)	1.2MB
3-1/2"	Double-sided Double-density (DS/DD)	720K
3-1/2"	Double-sided High-density (DS/HD)	1.44MB

Floppy Disk Handling Do's and Don'ts

Every beginning computer book contains a list of precautions telling you what *not* to do to a disk. Don't touch it here, don't touch it there, don't get it near any magnets, don't walk on it with spike heels. Blah blah blah. Although these are good warnings, by the time you get done reading them, you're too afraid to even pick up a disk.

A floppy disk drive can read disks that are equal to or less than the drive's own capacity. A high-capacity disk drive can read low-capacity disks, but the reverse will not work: a low-capacity disk drive cannot read high-capacity disks.

My recommendation is to chill out when it comes to disks. They're pretty sturdy, especially the 3 1/2-inch variety. Throw a disk across the room; it'll survive. Touch the exposed part (God forbid), and your data will probably remain intact. However, set an evil magnet on it overnight, and chances are the data will be gone in the morning.

Sticking a Floppy Disk in the Right Slot the Right Way

A disk will fit into a floppy drive in any number of ways: upside-down, sideways, even backwards. But a disk drive is like one of those dollar-change machines; if you don't insert the disk the right way, the drive won't be able to read it.

To insert the disk properly, hold the disk by its label, label facing up. Insert the disk into the drive, as shown in the picture. If the floppy drive has a lever or a door, close the door or flip the lever so it covers the slot.

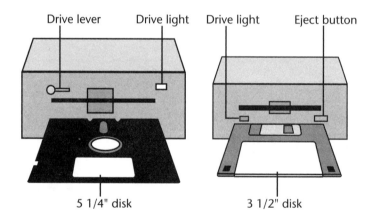

Drive lever   Drive light   Drive light   Eject button

A disk drive cannot read a disk unless the disk is inserted properly.

5 1/4" disk   3 1/2" disk

Pulling the Floppy Disk Out of the Slot

Before you pull the disk out of the disk drive, make sure the drive light is off. If the drive has an eject button, press the button, and the disk will pop out like a piece of toast. If the drive has a lever or door, flip the lever or open the door, and the disk will partially pop out. Gently pull the disk from the drive. Insert the disk into its pouch so the label faces out.

> **By the Way . . .**
>
> Pulling a disk out of its drive when the drive light is on is like pulling a record off the record machine when it's playing. If the drive light is on, the drive is reading or writing to the disk. If you pull the disk out, you might scramble the information on the disk or damage the disk and/or the read-write mechanism in the disk drive.

Making a Floppy Disk Useful

You get a brand-new box of disks. Can you use them to store information? Maybe. If the disks came *preformatted*, you can use them right out of the box. If they are not formatted, you'll have to do it yourself, with the help of DOS.

> You will normally format a disk only once: when it is brand new. If you format a disk that contains data, that data is erased during the formatting process. Before you format a disk, make sure the disk is blank or that it contains data you will never again need.

Formatting divides a disk into small storage areas and creates a *file allocation table* (FAT) on the disk. Whenever you save a file to disk, the parts of the file are saved in one or more of these storage areas. The FAT acts as a classroom seating chart, telling your computer the location of information in all of its storage areas.

Before You Begin

Before you start formatting disks, you have to ask yourself the following questions:

What kind of floppy disk drives do I have? What capacity is each disk drive? Is it high-density (1.2MB or 1.44MB) or double-density (360K or 720K)? The documentation that came with your computer will tell you whether you have high- or double-density drives.

What kind of floppy disks do I want to format? Do you have high-density or double-density disks? Check the disks or the box in which the disks came.

Why does this matter? There are two reasons. First, you cannot format a high-density disk in a double-density disk drive. For example, you cannot format a 1.2MB disk in a 360K drive.

Second, you can format a double-density disk in a high-density drive if you tell DOS specifically to do that. For example, you can format a 360K disk in a 1.2MB disk drive, if you know what you're doing.

Formatting a Disk in a Drive of the Same Capacity: Piece of Cake

If the capacity of your disk matches the capacity of your disk drive (for example, a 1.2MB disk in a 1.2MB disk drive), the formatting operation is fairly simple. Insert the disk in the drive and close the drive door. If the disk is in drive A, type **format a:** and press **Enter**. If the disk is in drive B, type **format b:** and press **Enter**.

Always follow the FORMAT command with the letter of the drive you want to use. With some versions of DOS, if you enter the FORMAT without specifying a drive letter, DOS will attempt to format drive C, your computer's hard drive.

When DOS is done formatting the disk, DOS asks if you want to give the disk a volume label. Type a volume label (up to 11 characters) and press Enter (or just press Enter if you don't want a volume label). (This volume label will appear whenever you display a file list for this disk.)

Formatting a Low-Density Disk in a High-Density Drive

If you want to format a low-density disk in a high-density drive (for example, a 360K disk in a 1.2MB disk drive), you need to add the /F switch to the FORMAT command to provide DOS with more detailed instructions. The /F switch allows you to specify the capacity of the formatted disk.

For example, to format a 360K disk in a 1.2MB drive, type **format a: /f:360** and press **Enter**. To format a 720K disk in a 1.44MB drive, type **format b: /f:720** and press **Enter**.

Inside the Belly of Your Computer: The Hard Disk

The hard disk drive is like a big floppy disk drive complete with disk (you don't take the disk out, it stays in the drive forever). To get information to the hard disk, you copy information to it from floppy disks or save the files you create directly to the hard disk. The information stays on the hard disk until you choose to erase the information. When the computer needs information, it goes directly to the hard disk, reads the information into memory, and continues working. You don't have to spoon-feed it floppies.

By the Way . . .

If you don't have a hard disk drive, you may as well be chiseling out your business letters on stone tablets. Most newer programs require that you have a hard disk in order to run them.

Don't Feed the Animals: Diskless Work Stations

If your computer is part of a network, it may not have any floppy disk drives or a hard disk drive. If that's the case, forget all this babble about floppy disks and hard disks. Your network probably has a *server* with a disk drive as big as an elephant that stores all the information and programs everyone in the company needs. A person called the *network administrator* acts as the zookeeper, feeding the server, making sure all the information you need is on hand, and keeping the server happy.

The Food on the Disks: Files

Information doesn't just roll around on a disk like marbles on a tile floor. Each packet of information is stored as a separate file that has its own name.

Your computer uses two types of files: data files and program files. Data files are the files you create and save—your business letters, reports, the pictures you draw, the results of any games you save. Program files are the files you get when you purchase a program. These files contain the instructions that tell your computer how to perform a task. A program may consist of a hundred or more program files.

Why Save Files onto a Disk?

When you begin typing information into your computer, the information initially consists of a flock of electronic blips flying around inside the computer. If you blow a fuse or accidentally turn off your computer, it's bye-bye blips, document and all. To keep from losing important information, you must store your work in a more stable location—on a disk.

Name That File

A disk full of files is like a house full of people. If all the people in the house were named Dave, there would be mass confusion whenever Dave got a phone call or letter. So each file needs a unique name.

Can you use any name? No, DOS has some rules you must follow when naming a file. The following guidelines should help:

☞ A filename consists of a *base name* (up to eight characters) and an optional *extension* (up to three characters)—for example, CHAPTER9.DOC.

☞ The base name and extension must be separated by a period.

☞ You cannot use any of the following characters:

" . / \ [ ] : * < > | + ; , ? space

(You can use the period to separate the base name and extension, but nowhere else.)

☞ Although you cannot use spaces, you can be tricky and use the underline character (_) to represent a space.

☞ Many programs will automatically add an extension for you. For example, when you name a file in Microsoft Word, the program automatically adds the .DOC extension.

What's Wrong with This Picture?

The following list contains correct and incorrect file names. Cross out any incorrect file names and explain why each file name is correct or incorrect:

1. CH09XT.LT

Reason:

2. FRANK&LOU.LTR

Reason:

3. CHAP10.

Reason:

4. .DOC

Reason:

5. LUNCH?.MEM

Reason:

6. CH.10.DOC

Reason:

7. CHAP 10.DOC

Reason:

8. CHAP_05.WPF

Reason:

Answers:

1. Correct: A file name can contain fewer than eight characters and can include numbers. The extension can be fewer than three characters.

2. Incorrect: The & sign is okay, but the file name is nine characters long (one too many). The extension is okay.

3. Correct: The file name is okay. Extensions are optional; you don't have to use one.

4. Incorrect: Although you can use a file name without an extension, you cannot use an extension without a file name.

5. Incorrect: You cannot use a question mark in a file name.

6. Incorrect: You can use only one period in a file name: to separate the file name and extension. This file name uses two periods.

7. Incorrect: You cannot use spaces in a file name.

8. Correct: You can use an underline character in a file name.

Keeping Tabs on Your Files

A single hard disk can store hundreds or thousands of files all elbowing each other for a peek at the parade. It's great that disks can hold so much information, but disks can get crowded, making it mighty difficult to pick out a familiar face. To keep files from getting lost, you must keep them organized.

Organizing Files on Floppy Disks: No Problem

Organizing files on a floppy disk is not all that difficult, because you normally don't store very many files per disk. Even if you store as many as 30 files on a single disk, you can manage to search through a list of files fairly quickly.

Even so, you should follow three standard procedures to make the information more accessible:

Give each file a descriptive name. This name should help you remember what's in the file. For example, JOHNSON.LTR tells you the name of the person the document concerns (Johnson) and the type of document (LTR for Letter).

Label your disks. Label each disk with the names of the files stored on that disk and the date. That way, you'll know what's on the disk and which disk holds the most recent revisions.

Keep disks uncluttered. Copy any files you don't use very often to separate disks and store them in a safe place. Copy the files you use most often to a separate set of disks, and keep these disks handy.

Getting Your Act Together with Directories

Because hard disks can store thousands of files, you need to create *directories* and *subdirectories* to help organize your files. To understand directories, think of your disk as a city. All your files are like little houses inside the city. Directories are like postal zones, grouping the files to make them easier to locate. In this analogy, a directory name is like a ZIP code. Whenever you are looking for a file, you can use the directory name to help you determine the file's general location.

> ## By the Way . . .
> Some users like to create directories on their floppy disks. Although I think this is a bit much, it can be done.

Shaking Your Directory Tree

Directories and subdirectories form a structure, that looks like a family tree. This tree structure is standard to many file-management programs, including DOS, so you will soon get tired of seeing it.

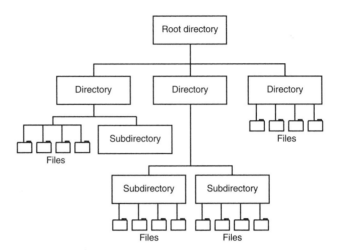

A directory tree illustrates how a hard disk is organized.

To understand how your computer locates files, it's helpful to look at the directory tree in terms of a *path*. Whenever you tell your computer where a file is located, you're essentially telling it to follow a specific path through the directory tree. For example, you may need to tell your computer to get the CUB file that's in subdirectory LION, in the directory ZOO, on drive C. The path would be c:\zoo\lion\cub.

Once you get accustomed to using directories, they're pretty straightforward; just weave through your directory tree to your destination.

The Least You Need to Know

In this chapter, I've given you a lot to chew on. Make sure the following stuff sticks to your ribs:

☞ Most computers have three disk drives: A and B (the floppy drives) and C (the hard drive).

☞ There are four types of floppy disks: 5 1/4" double-density (360K), 5 1/4" high-density (1.2MB), 3 1/2" double-density (720K), and 3 1/2" high-density (1.44MB).

- ☞ Take good care of your floppy disks.

- ☞ A high-density floppy disk drive can read high-density and low-density disks, but a low-density disk drive can read only low-density disks.

- ☞ Do not pull a floppy disk out of a drive when the drive light is lit.

- ☞ Whenever you create something on the computer, you should save it in a file on disk.

- ☞ When saving files on a hard disk, you should save groups of related files in separate directories.

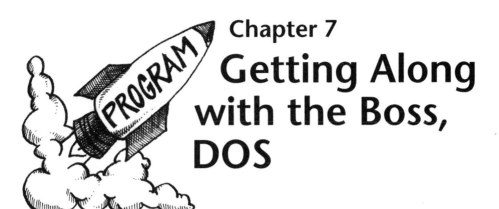

Chapter 7

Getting Along with the Boss, DOS

In This Chapter

- ☞ Coming face-to-face with the DOS prompt
- ☞ How to tell DOS what to do
- ☞ Using DOS to see what's on a disk
- ☞ Using DOS to change to a directory and view the contents of the directory
- ☞ How to run a program from the DOS prompt
- ☞ How to copy, delete, and rename files
- ☞ Common DOS messages and what they mean

Think of DOS as the boss, or the supervisor, of your computer. As any good boss, DOS does most of its work in the background. You just run the program you want to use and then use the program to perform your tasks. DOS works behind the curtains to make sure everything goes according to plan.

Occasionally, however, you have to work directly with DOS. In this chapter, you will learn what you need to know when you come face-to-face with DOS.

Facing the DOS Prompt

When you boot your computer, DOS displays a prompt (C:>, C>, A>, or something similar), showing the letter of the active drive and telling you that you can enter a command. It doesn't tell you much else. To enter a command, you must type it at the prompt and press the **Enter** key.

But what do you type and how do you type it? In the next few sections, you will learn the most commonly used DOS commands and the correct way to enter them.

A DOS command is an order that you tell DOS to carry out. There are two types of DOS commands: *internal* and *external*. Internal commands, such as DIR, are stored in memory for quick access. External commands, such as FOR-MAT, are small programs that are stored on disk. When you enter an external command, DOS runs the program required to perform the task.

Harmless DOS Commands, Just for Practice

Before you get into the heavy, important DOS commands where mistakes do count, try a few light commands that can't hurt anything.

What's Today's Date?

Your computer probably has an internal, battery-powered clock that keeps track of the date and time. To tell DOS to display the date on-screen, gather your courage and type **date** and press **Enter**. DOS will display something like:

> **Current date is Tue 06-01-93**
> **Enter new date:**

If the date is correct, press **Enter**. If the date is incorrect, type the correct date in the form mm-dd-yy (for example, 07-04-93 for July 4, 1993) and press **Enter**.

What Version of DOS Do You Have?

Every time Microsoft Corporation or some other maker of DOS releases an updated version of DOS, the version number increases, and the program can do more new things or can do old things better. Hence, DOS 5.0 is better than DOS 4.01.

To find out which version of DOS is installed on your computer, type

ver   6.00

and press **Enter** (VER stands for "version"). DOS displays the version number on-screen. Write down the version number and keep it next to your computer. (You'll need to know it later.)

When you type a DOS command, you don't have to worry about capitalization: date, DATE, and dAte are all the same to DOS. However, if you leave out a space, add too many spaces, or use punctuation marks that we don't tell you to use, DOS will not recognize the command. For example, if you typed **date.** and pressed **Enter**, DOS would display the message **Invalid date.**

Sweeping Up the Screen

Now that you have the date, time, and DOS version number displayed on-screen, your screen should be looking pretty cluttered. To clear the screen, type **cls** and press **Enter**. (CLS stands for CLear Screen.)

Giving DOS a Makeover

The DOS prompt normally shows only the letter of the active disk drive (for example, A>, B>, or C>). You can change the look of the DOS prompt by using the PROMPT command. Try typing a few of the prompt commands from the following list:

☞ Type **prompt nq** and press **Enter**. $n displays the current drive, and $q displays the equal sign (=). The prompt should now look like C=.

SPEAK LIKE A GEEK

Keep in mind that a *drive* is the device that reads information from disks. (DOS refers to the various drives as A, B, and C.) A *directory* is a division of the drive that stores a bunch of related files.

If you get a prompt you don't like, simply type **prompt** and press **Enter**. The prompt will return to the way it was before you started messing with it. If that doesn't work, press **Ctrl+Alt+Del** to warm boot your computer.

☛ Type **prompt $v nb** and press **Enter**. $v displays the DOS version number, and $b displays a vertical line called the pipe symbol (|). The prompt should now look something like **MS-DOS Version 5.0 C|** (though why you would want a prompt like this is beyond me).

☛ Type **prompt pg** and press **Enter**. $p displays the current drive letter and name of the directory you are in, and $g displays a right angle bracket (>). The prompt should now look something like C:\>. (This is one of the most commonly used prompts. The backslash by itself stands for the root directory.)

When you are done fooling around, type **prompt pg** and press **Enter**. The remaining commands in this chapter assume that you will be able to see the drive and directory names at the DOS prompt.

Where Have All the Files Gone?

You will use DOS mostly to work with files. You will run program files, copy files from one disk to another, delete files to keep your disks uncluttered, and so on. Whenever you work with files, you must tell DOS where those files are located. In the upcoming sections, you will learn how to specify the drive and directory where files are stored.

Changing to a Disk Drive: The Old Shell Game

To change to a disk drive, type the letter of the drive followed by a colon (:) and then press **Enter**. For example, if you have a disk in drive A, type **a:** and press **Enter**. The DOS prompt then changes to A:\>. To change back to drive C, type **c:** and press **Enter**.

Changing to a Directory: Another Shell Game

When DOS activates a disk drive, DOS automatically looks for files in the first directory on the disk: the *root directory*. If the files are in a different directory, you must change to that directory by entering the CHDIR or CD (Change Directory) command. In the next few sections, you will change back and forth between directories to get a feel for it.

Before you change to a disk drive, make sure the drive contains a formatted disk (your hard disk and the program disks you purchase are already formatted). If you change to a drive that does not contain a formatted disk, the following error message will appear:

Not ready reading drive A Abort, Retry, Fail?

Insert a formatted disk in the drive, close the drive door, and press **R** for Retry.

Going to the House of DOS: The DOS Directory

Depending on how your computer is set up, you may have to change to the DOS directory to enter a DOS command. Before you change to the DOS directory, make sure drive C is active; type **c:** and press **Enter**. The prompt C:\> appears on-screen. Type **cd \dos** and press **Enter** (CD stands for Change Directory). The prompt C:\DOS> appears on-screen. You are now in the house of DOS.

Going Back to the Root Cellar

To change back to the root directory, type **cd ** and press **Enter**. The DOS prompt changes back to C:\>.

> ## By the Way . . .
> The root directory contains a lot of important files, so don't play around too much in this directory. I once moved all the files in the root directory to the DOS directory (to tidy things up), and couldn't get my computer to boot. Took me three days to recover.

Changing to a Subdirectory

Say you want to work with the files in a subdirectory (a directory that's under another directory). For example, suppose you want to work with the files in C:\DATA\BOOKS. You can change to the subdirectory in either of two ways.

The first way is to enter two CD commands. First, you would type **cd \data** to change to C:\DATA. (The backslash \ tells DOS to start at the root directory.) Then, you would type **cd books** to change to C:\DATA\BOOKS. (Note that the backslash is omitted here, because you don't want to start back at the root directory.)

The other way to change to a subdirectory is to use a single CD command followed by a complete list of directories that lead to the subdirectory. Type **cd \data\books** and press **Enter**.

So What's in This Directory?

Once you have changed to the drive and directory that contains the files you want to work with, you can view a list of the files on that drive and directory. To view a list of files, type **dir** and press **Enter**. A file list appears.

Whoa! Slowing Down the File List

If the file list contains too many files to fit on one screen, the list scrolls off the top of the screen, making you feel as though you are falling very fast.

To prevent the list from scrolling off the screen, type **dir /w** and press **Enter**. The /W (wide) switch tells DOS to display only the names of the files and to display the file names in several columns across the screen.

Another way to slow down the list is to use the /P (pause) switch. Type **dir /p** and press **Enter**. DOS displays only one screenful of file names at a time. You can press any key to see the next screenful of names.

Narrowing the File List

You may not want to view all the files in a directory. You may, for example, want to view only those files that have the .EXE extension or the .COM extension. To view a group of files, you can use *wild-card characters*.

Here are some ways you can use wild-card entries with the DIR command:

Type **dir *.com** and press **Enter** to view a list of all files with the .COM file name extension (for example, HELP.COM, EDIT.COM, and TREE.COM).

Type **dir ???.*** and press **Enter** to view a list of all files that have a file name of three letters or fewer (for example, EGA.SYS, SYS.COM, and FC.EXE).

A *wild-card character* is any character that takes the place of another character or a group of characters. Think of a wild-card character as a wild card in a game of poker. If the Joker is wild, you can use it in place of any card in the entire deck of cards. In DOS, you can use two wild characters: a question mark (?) and an asterisk (*). The question mark stands in for any single character. The asterisk stands in for any group of characters.

Type **dir s???.*** and press **Enter** to view a list of all files whose file name starts with S and has four letters or fewer (for example, SORT.EXT and SYS.COM).

By the Way . . .

You can use a wild-card entry with a switch. For example, if you type **dir *.com /w** and press **Enter**, DOS will display only those files with the .COM extension and will display them in several columns across the screen.

Ditching DOS: Running Another Program

The easiest way to deal with DOS is to avoid it; run one of your applications and have DOS retreat backstage where it belongs.

To run an application from DOS, first change to the drive and directory where the program's files are stored. For example, say you want to run WordPerfect, and the WordPerfect files are in C:\WP51. You would change to the C drive and then type **cd \wp51** and press **Enter**.

Next, type the command required to run the program and then press **Enter**. For example, to run WordPerfect, you would type **wp** and press **Enter**. (The documentation that came with the program will tell you what to type. Table 7.1 lists commands for popular programs.)

The program starts and displays a screen or menu where you can start working.

Table 7.1   Try the Following Commands for Some of the More Popular Programs

To run this program	Type this command and press Enter
America Online	**aol**
Carmen Sandiego	**carmen**
dBASE	**dbase**
Harvard Graphics	**hg**
Lotus 1-2-3	**123**
Microsoft Windows	**win**
Microsoft Word	**word**
Microsoft Works	**works**
Paradox	**paradox**
PC Tools	**pcshell** OR **pctools**
PFS: First Choice	**first**
PFS: First Publisher	**fp**
Prodigy	**prodigy**
Professional Write	**pw**
Q&A	**qa**
Quattro Pro	**q**

To run this program	Type this command and press Enter
Quicken	**q**
TurboTax	**ttax**
WordPerfect	**wp**
WordStar	**ws**

By the Way . . .

If you misplaced your documentation, turn to Chapter 19 for a discussion of how to survive without documentation. Chapter 19 will tell you how to figure out what command you need to enter to run a program.

Getting Organized with Directories

Early in this chapter, you learned how to change to the DOS directory. The DOS directory was created by the DOS setup program when DOS was installed. However, you may want to create your own directories for storing other program files or the files you create. The following sections tell you how to create and delete directories.

Let's Make a Directory

To make a directory, you use the DOS MKDIR or MD (Make Directory) command followed by the name you want to give to the directory. First, type **c:** and press **Enter**, and then type **cd ** and press **Enter**. This puts you at the root directory of drive C. Type **md funnydir** and press **Enter**. You now have a directory called FUNNYDIR on your disk. Type **cd \funnydir** and press **Enter** to change to the FUNNYDIR directory. Easy stuff!

OOPS!

You can't use just any name for a directory. A directory name can consist of up to eight characters with a three character extension (just like a file name). You can use any characters except the following:

" . / \ [ ] : * < > | + ; , ?

And don't use the extension—it'll just complicate things later.

Let's Nuke a Directory

Having too many directories can be as confusing as having all your files lumped into one. To remove a directory at the DOS prompt, you must use the RMDIR or RD command, both of which stand for Remove Directory. I use RD because it's shorter.

To nuke a directory, you first have to be in the directory that is just above the directory you want to nuke. In the case of FUNNYDIR, this is the root directory. To push the button on FUNNYDIR, type **cd ** and press **Enter**. Then type **rd funnydir** and press **Enter**. FUNNYDIR is history. Try changing to it if you don't believe me.

DOS will not allow you to remove a directory that contains files or sub-directories. To remove the directory, you must first delete all its files and sub-directories or move the files to another directory or disk. You'll learn how to do all that later.

Taking Control of Your Files

I hope all the talk early in this chapter about disks and directories did not blur your focus on what really matters—files. Without files, there would be no need for disks or directories in which to store them. In the upcoming sections, you'll learn how to copy, delete, and rename files.

Cloning Files

One of the most common file management tasks is to copy files from one disk or directory to another. For example, you may copy files from your hard disk to a floppy disk to share the files with a colleague.

By the Way . . .

Before you can copy files to a directory, you must have created the directory. If you try to copy a file to a directory that does not exist, DOS will display an error message.

To copy a file from one disk or directory to another, first change to the drive and directory that contains the files you want to copy. Then, type **copy file1.ext d:\directory**, where *file1.ext* is the name of the file you want to copy, and *d:\directory* is the drive and directory to which you want the file copied. (See the examples listed in Table 7.2.) Press **Enter**. DOS copies the file.

Table 7.2   Sample Copy Commands

Command	What it does
copy *.doc a:	Copies all files that have the .DOC extension from the current directory to the disk in drive A.
copy chap09.doc b:	Copies only the file named CHAP09.DOC from the current directory to the disk in Drive B.
copy *.doc c:\samples	Copies all files that have the .DOC extension from the current directory to a directory named C:\SAMPLES.
copy *.* c:\samples\books	Copies all files from the current directory to C:\SAMPLES\BOOKS.
copy chap09.* c:\samples	Copies all files named CHAP09 (CHAP09.DOC, CHAP09.BAK, etc.) from the current directory to C:\SAMPLES.

Zapping Files

If you are sure you no longer need a file, you can delete the file from a disk in order to prevent the disk from becoming cluttered. However, before you delete a file, make sure you will no longer need it; you may not be able to get the file back.

To delete a single file, change to the drive and directory that contains the file you want to delete. Type **del filename.ext**, where *filename.ext* is the name of the file you want to delete. Press **Enter**. DOS deletes the file.

TECHNO NERD TEACHES

A typical DOS command, as shown here

copy c:\data\ johnson.ltr b: /v

consists of the following elements:

Command   This is the name of the DOS command (in this case, COPY). It tells DOS which action you want DOS to carry out.

Delimiters   Delimiters are spaces and special characters (such as /, \, and :) that break down the command line for DOS. Think of delimiters as the spaces between words in a sentence.

Parameters   Parameters specify the objects on which you want DOS to perform the action. In the example above, c:\data\johnson.ltr is the parameter.

Switches   Switches allow you to control how the command performs its action. In this case, the /V switch tells DOS to verify the copy operation to make sure the copy matches the original.

You can delete a group of files by using wild-card characters. For example, to delete all files that have the .BAK extension, you would change to the drive and directory where those files are stored and enter **del *.bak**. To delete all files in a directory (which you must do, remember, before you can remove a directory), change to that directory and enter **del *.***.

Renaming Files

There may be times when you need to rename a file or a group of files, perhaps to make the names more descriptive or to avoid name conflicts with other files.

To rename files, change to the drive and directory that contains the file you want to rename. Type **ren file1.ext file2.ext**, where *file1.ext* is the name of the file you want to rename, and *file2.ext* is the new name for the file. Press **Enter**. DOS renames the file.

You can rename a group of files by using wild-card characters. For example, say you want to change the file name extension for a group of files from .DOC to .TXT. You would change to the drive and directory where those files are stored and enter **ren *.doc *.txt**.

There Must Be a Better Way: The DOS Shell

If you have DOS version 4.0 or later (preferably version 5.0 or later), you have a program called the *DOS Shell*, which gives DOS a friendlier face. Instead of typing commands and file names at the DOS prompt, you can select files from a list and choose commands from menus. I won't go into the gory details about the shell in this book. (But you can learn more by getting *The Complete Idiot's Guide to DOS.*)

By the Way . . .

To find out if you have the DOS Shell, change to the DOS directory, type **dosshell**, and press **Enter**. You can use a mouse in the shell, so try poking around to see what you can find. When you want to leave the shell, press **Alt+F** to open the file menu, and then press **X** for Exit.

Common DOS Messages in Plain English

As you work in DOS, you may come across some error messages and warnings and wonder what they mean. The following sections translate the DOS messages you're most likely to encounter.

All files in directory will be deleted
Are you sure (Y/N)?

You probably entered the **delete *.*** command at the DOS prompt. This tells DOS to delete all the files on the current drive or directory. If you are sure you want to do this, press **Y**. If you don't want to delete all the files, press **N**.

Bad command or file name

DOS usually displays this message if you have a typo in the command you entered. Check to make sure the command is typed correctly.

If the command is typed correctly, maybe DOS cannot find the command's program file. For example, you may have to be in the DOS directory to use the DOS FORMAT command. In such a case, you must change to the directory that contains the program file before you can run the file.

File cannot be copied onto itself

You will get this message if you try to copy a file into the same directory that already contains the file. If you want to create a copy of a file in the same directory, you have to give the copy a new name.

File not found

You will get this message if you try to copy, delete, rename, or perform some other operation on a file that does not exist or on a file that is in a different location from where you think it is.

If you get this message, make sure you typed the file name correctly. If the file name is okay, change to the drive and directory where you think the file is stored and use the DIR command to view a list of files. See if the file is where you think it is.

Insufficient disk space

DOS displays this error message when you try to copy more files to a disk than the disk can hold. If you get this error message, you may need to copy the files to more than one disk.

Non-system disk or disk error
Replace and press any key when ready

You may get this error message when you boot your computer. Usually it means that you left a disk in drive A. Simply remove the disk and press any key to continue.

If you normally boot from a floppy disk, you may have forgotten to insert the DOS startup disk in drive A. Insert the DOS startup disk, close the drive door, and press any key.

Not ready reading drive A
Abort, Retry, Fail?

You will usually get this message for one of these reasons:

☞ You forgot to put a disk in drive A. Insert a disk, close the drive door, and press **R** for Retry.

☞ You forgot to close the drive door. Close the drive door and press **R** for Retry.

☞ The disk in drive A is not formatted. If a brand-new, never-been-formatted disk is in drive A, DOS will not be able to read the disk. Insert a formatted disk into drive A, close the drive door, and press **R**.

☞ If you changed to drive A by mistake, press **F** for Fail or **A** for Abort. This tells DOS to stop looking to drive A. A message appears telling you that drive A is no longer valid. Type **c:** and press **Enter** to return to drive C.

☞ If you have a double-density drive and put a high-density disk in the drive.

The Least You Need to Know

Although you don't need to know everything about DOS in order to use a computer, the more you know, the easier it will be for you to get out of trouble. In this chapter, I have tried to teach you as much as possible without teaching too much. The following list provides important information to help you review.

☞ The DOS prompt indicates the current drive and tells you that you can enter a command.

☞ To change to a disk drive, type the drive letter followed by a colon, and press **Enter**. For example, type **a:** and press **Enter**.

☞ To change to a directory, type **cd \dirname** (where *dirname* is the name of the directory) and press **Enter**.

continues

continued

☞ To view a list of files in a directory, type **dir** and press **Enter.**

☞ To run a program from the DOS prompt, change to the drive and directory that contains the program's files, type the command to run the program, and press **Enter.**

☞ To format a floppy disk, insert a blank disk in drive A or B, type **format a:** or **format b:**, and press **Enter.**

☞ To make a directory, change to the directory under which you want the new directory created. Type **md dirname** (where *dirname* is the name you want to give the directory) and press **Enter.**

☞ To copy a file from one disk or directory to another, change to the disk and directory that contains the file you want to copy. Type **copy file1.ext d:\directory**, where *file1.ext* is the name of the file you want to copy, and *d:\directory* is the drive and directory where you want the file copied.

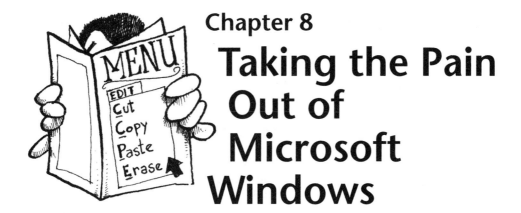

Chapter 8

Taking the Pain Out of Microsoft Windows

In This Chapter

- ☛ Microsoft Windows—What it is and why you should know about it

- ☛ Getting into and out of Windows

- ☛ How to get around in Windows

- ☛ Using the programs that come with Windows

- ☛ Working with Windows icons and running programs

- ☛ How to use the mouse to snoop around in Windows

It's no secret that DOS isn't very friendly. It gives you the evil eye, daring you to do something useful. In this chapter, you will learn about a *graphical user interface*, called Microsoft Windows, that is designed to make your computer easier to use. (Graphical user interface is commonly abbreviated GUI, which is pronounced "gooey.")

Some people, not me of course, joke that GUI actually stands for *graphical unfriendly interface*. As with most jokes, this one has some truth; before Windows can make your computer easier to use, you have to know how to get around in Windows. In this chapter, you'll learn what you need to know.

Why Windows?

At this point, you may be saying, "Joe, why would I want to run *another* program on top of DOS before running the program I will actually use." Fair enough: I'll give you two good reasons.

Okay, I lied, I'll give you a third reason for running Windows. It allows you to *multitask*—to have one program performing a task in the background while you use another program. Some programs, such as the DOS Shell, allow you to switch between two or more programs (task-switching) but do not allow a program to perform operations in the background (multitasking).

First, Windows allows you to learn new programs faster. Most Windows programs use a standard menu system. Once you learn how to use the menus in one program, learning to use the menus in any Windows program is a snap. For example, to save a file in most Windows programs, you pull down the File menu and select **S**ave.

Second, everybody is doing Windows. I know, I know, just because everybody else is doing it is no reason for you to do it, but most companies that are making new programs are making those programs to run in Windows. So if you want to use the latest, greatest programs, you will have to have Windows running on your computer.

SPEAK LIKE A GEEK

The Program Manager is the head honcho in Windows. When you start Windows, the Program Manager runs automatically and allows you to run your other programs. When you run a program, the Program Manager retreats to the background.

Kick-Starting Windows

Before you can take advantage of Windows' ease-of-use, you have to start it from the DOS prompt. To start Windows, change to the drive and directory that contains the Windows files. (Type **c:** and press **Enter**; then type **cd \windows** and press **Enter**.) Then type **win** and press **Enter**. The Windows title screen appears for a few moments, and then you see the Windows Program Manager.

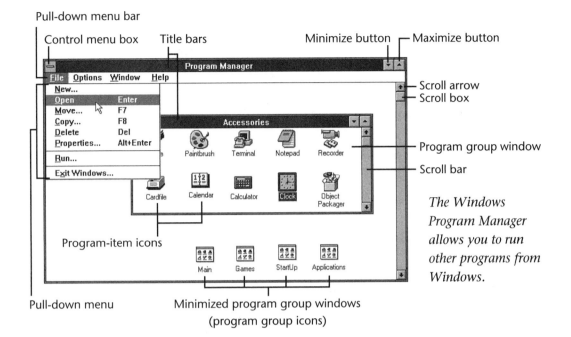

Pull-down menu bar

Control menu box   Title bars   Minimize button ┌ Maximize button

Scroll arrow
Scroll box

Program group window

Scroll bar

*The Windows
Program Manager
allows you to run
other programs from
Windows.*

Program-item icons

Pull-down menu   Minimized program group windows
(program group icons)

Climbing Out of Windows

The first thing you should know about any
program, including Windows, is how to get
out of the program. To get out of Windows,
double-click on the control menu box (in the
upper-left corner of the Program Manager
window). A message appears, asking if you're
sure you want to leave. Press **Enter**.

If you try to exit Windows
before saving your work,
Windows will display a
message asking if you want
to save your work before
leaving. After you save your
work, Windows will let you
leave.

Windows Anatomy 101

Okay, now that you just got out of Windows, get back in. When you're
back in the Program Manager, you may start to wonder what all those
things on the screen are for. Those are the things that make your computer
easier to use. Let's take a tour right now.

First, notice that each window has a *title bar*, a headline at the top of the window. It gives the name of the window or program and sometimes the name of the file that's open.

The Program Manager contains one or more *program group windows*, each of which contains a group of *program-item icons*. A program-item icon is a small picture that represents a program. Double-click on one of the icons now. A window should open. Double-click on the box in the upper left corner of the window to zap it.

See the two buttons in the upper right corner of the Program Manager window? The one on the left is the *minimize* button. It shrinks the window down to a mere icon. Go ahead, click on it. Now, double-click on the icon to restore it to full-size again. The button on the right is the *maximize* button. It enlarges the window to take up the whole screen. Click on it. The button then changes to a double-headed *restore* button, which allows you to return the window to its original size.

At the upper left corner of every window is a *control menu box*. Selecting this box opens a menu which allows you to close the window or change its size and location. If you double-click on this button, you close the window, and quit the program.

Just below the title bar of the Program Manager window is a *pull-down menu bar*. This bar contains a list of the pull-down menus available. Each menu contains a list of related commands. Click on **Window** to open the Window menu. Click on it again to close the menu. You'll come across pull-down menu bars in all Windows programs.

If a window contains more information than can be displayed in the window, a *scroll bar* appears. You can use the scroll bars to view the contents of the window that are not currently shown on-screen. You'll learn how to use a scroll bar later.

The Windows Bonus Pack

In addition to making your computer easier to use, Windows comes with several useful programs. Table 8.1 lists the programs you're likely to find most useful as you toil away at your computer. (These programs are automatically installed when you install Windows.)

Table 8.1   Programs That Come with Microsoft Windows

Program	What it does
	Accessories Program Group
Write	This is a generic word-processing program that lets you type and print documents, such as letters and reports. Write offers several features that let you style the text. You'll probably want something more advanced.
Notepad	This is a no-frills text editor that lets you create simple documents.
Cardfile	The Cardfile acts as a self-sorting Rolodex. You can use it to keep track of names, addresses, phone numbers, recipes, or any other information.
Calculator	The Calculator works just like a hand-held calculator.
Terminal	Use the terminal with a modem to connect and communicate with other computers that have modems.
	Main Program Group
Clipboard	The Clipboard acts as a holding area for text or graphics. Whenever you cut or copy something from one program, it is placed on the clipboard. You can then paste it elsewhere in the document or in some other document.
	Games Program Group
Games	Windows 3.0 comes with two games: Solitaire and Reversi. Windows 3.1 comes with an additional game called Minesweeper.

You are not limited to the programs that come with Windows. Many software companies create programs that run under Windows and have the same look and feel as all Windows programs.

> ### By the Way . . .
> The Solitaire game that comes with Windows is good practice for learning how to use the mouse. You can tell your boss I said so.

Learning the Ropes: Getting Around in Windows

If you want to use Windows, get a mouse. Trying to use Windows without a mouse is like trying to type with mittens on. Chapter 5 explains common mouse techniques: pointing, clicking, double-clicking, and so on. The next few sections explain how to use the mouse to perform common tasks in Windows, including running programs and selecting commands from pull-down menus.

Opening the Magical Mystery Box

In the upper left corner of every window is a small box (the *control menu box*) that hides some mighty important commands. When you click on this box, a menu appears that allows you to close the window or change the size or position of the window. Select an option from the menu and then follow the on-screen messages to complete the operation.

Take Your Pick: Using a Pull-Down Menu

Pull-down menus work like control menu boxes. You click on the menu's name to pull it down from the menu bar, and then you click on the command you want to enter.

Conversing with Windows Through Dialog Boxes

Some commands on the pull-down menus are followed by an ellipses (...). This shows that if you select the command, a dialog box will appear. Think of it as a trip to the service desk at a department store. You go up and ask for something, and the person behind the desk hands you a form to fill out. A dialog box is basically a form used to tell the program exactly what you want.

Pull-down menus are a way of conserving screen space. The menu remains hidden in the menu bar until you need an option. When you are done selecting an option, the menu retreats back into the menu bar.

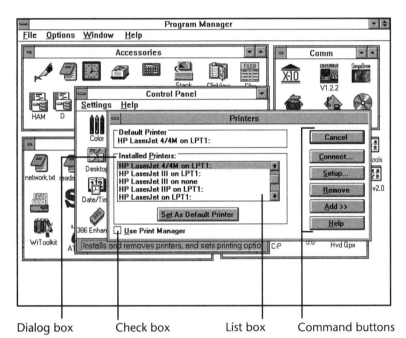

A dialog box is Windows' way of asking for more information.

Dialog box   Check box   List box   Command buttons

A dialog box may request that you type an entry in a *text box*, or select one or more items from a *list box*. Some dialog boxes contain *drop-down lists*. With a drop-down list, only one item is shown. To see the rest of the items, you must click on the down arrow to the right of the list box.

Dialog boxes may also contain a set of *check-box* options (little boxes) and *option buttons* (little round things) that you can select. With check-box options, you click on an option to turn it on or off (you can select more than one option in a group). With option buttons, you click on an option to turn it on. To turn an option off, you select a different option in the group (you can select only one option in a group).

Once you have made your selections in the dialog box, you must click on one of the *command buttons* to execute your choices. Most dialog boxes have at least two command buttons—one to give your final OK, and another to cancel your selections.

Seeing More with Scroll Bars

Think of a window as, well, a window. When you look through a window, you don't see everything that's on the other side of the window. You see only a portion of it.

A Windows window is the same. If a window cannot display everything it contains, a scroll bar will appear along the right side and/or bottom of the window. You can use the scroll bar to bring the hidden contents of the window into view.

To scroll the contents of a window, you can click on the *scroll arrows* at either end of the bar. Click once on an arrow to scroll incrementally in the direction of the arrow. Hold down the mouse button on an arrow to scroll continuously in that direction.

To scroll more quickly, use the *scroll box* inside the scroll bar. Move the mouse pointer over the scroll box, hold down the mouse button, and drag the box to the area of the window you want to view. For example, to move to the middle of the window's contents, drag the scroll box to the middle of the bar. You can also click inside the scroll bar on either side of the scroll box to move one screenful at a time.

Launching Programs from Windows

You can run a program from Windows in either of two ways, depending on whether or not the program has a corresponding icon. In the next couple of sections, you'll learn how to run programs with or without icons.

Icon Do It: Running a Program with an Icon

Every Windows program has a corresponding program-item icon that you can use to run the program. In addition, when you install Windows, it searches for any non-Windows programs and creates icons for those programs.

If a program has an icon, here's how to run it. Change to the program-group window that contains the program's icon, as explained earlier. If necessary, use the scroll bar to bring the program's icon into view. Then double-click on the program's icon. A program window opens, allowing you to use the program.

Anyone Can Do It: Running a Program without an Icon

If you installed a DOS program after installing Windows or if the Windows installation program did not create an icon for one of your DOS programs, you can still run the program from Windows.

To start, click on **File** in the Program Manager's pull-down menu bar. When you see the File menu, click on **Run**.

Type a complete path to the directory in which the program's files are stored followed by the name of the file that executes the program. For example, type **c:\word5\word.exe**. Press **Enter** or click on **OK**.

SPEAK LIKE A GEEK

A *Windows program* is a program that has been especially written to run under Microsoft Windows. It looks like Microsoft Windows, and it can take advantage of all the benefits of Windows. A *non-Windows program (DOS program)* is a program you can run from the DOS prompt or from Windows. It does not have the look and feel of Windows, and it cannot take full advantage of the Windows features.

In Windows 3.1, when you choose Run from the File menu, the dialog box that appears contains a **Browse** button. Click on the button and you get a list of directories and files on your hard disk. You can poke around in the directories to find the program you want to run.

If you cannot see the desired window, click on **Window** in the pull-down menu bar and then select the name of the window you want to go to. The selected window is then moved to the front and is activated. If that doesn't work, press **Ctrl+Esc** and then choose the window from the Task List.

Dealing with Windows

Working in Windows is like being the dealer in a game of cards. Whenever you start a program or maximize an icon, a new window appears on-screen, overlapping the other windows. Open enough windows, and pretty soon your screen looks like you've just dealt a hand of 52-card pickup. The following sections tell you how to clean up the mess.

Moving a Window to the Top of the Deck

If you can see any part of a window, the easiest way to move the window to the top of the stack is to click on the exposed portion of the window. The window automatically jumps up front and covers anything under it.

Fanning Your Cards

When you're holding a handful of cards, you want to see what you have, so you fan the cards. In Windows, you can view a portion of each window on-screen by using a similar technique. You can tell Windows to display the windows side-by-side (*tiled*) or overlapping (*cascade*). Here's how: Click on **Window** in the pull-down menu bar and click on **Cascade** or **Tile**.

Although cascaded windows overlap, you can see the title bar of each window, so you can quickly switch to a window by clicking on its title bar.

A Fancy Card Trick: Resizing a Window

As you are rearranging windows on-screen, you may want to shrink windows that are less important or that contain fewer icons, or you may want to enlarge more important windows.

Start by moving the mouse pointer to the edge or corner of the window until the pointer turns into a double-headed arrow. (Use an edge to change only one dimension of the window. Use a corner to change two dimensions, for example width and height.)

Hold down the mouse button and drag the pointer toward the center of the window to make it smaller or away from the center to make it larger. Release the button, and voilà!

Dragging a Window Across the Screen

As you size and resize windows, you will probably want to move your windows around. The process is simple. Move the mouse pointer into the window's title bar. While holding down the mouse button, roll the mouse on your desk until the window is where you want it. Release the mouse button, and the window is anchored in position.

What About My Keyboard?

No, your keyboard isn't obsolete just yet. Although Windows works best with a mouse, you can still use your keyboard. The keyboard shortcuts listed in Table 8.2 explain how.

Table 8.2   Windows Keyboard Shortcuts

Press	To
Alt+Esc	Cycle through the application windows and icons.
Ctrl+F6 (or Ctrl+Tab)	Cycle through program group icons and windows.

continues

Table 8.2   Continued

Press	To
Alt+Spacebar	Open the Control menu for an application window or icon.
Alt+- (hyphen)	Open the Control menu for a program group window or icon.
Arrow keys	Move from one icon to another in the active program group window.
Alt (or F10)	Activate the pull-down menu bar.
Alt+selection letter	Open a pull-down menu from the menu bar or select an option in a dialog box.
Enter	Run the application whose icon is highlighted, or restore a window that's been reduced to an icon.
Esc	Close a menu or dialog box.
Ctrl+Esc	View the task list, which allows you to switch to a different application.
F1	Get help.
Ctrl+F4	Minimize the selected program group window.
Alt+F4	Exit the active application or exit Windows.

Put It to Work

Now that you know the Windows basics, try using what you learned to create your own program-group window. You can drag the icons for the programs you use most often into this window for convenient access:

- ☛ Press **Ctrl+Esc** to display the Task List.

- ☛ Use the arrow keys to highlight Program Manager, and press **Enter**. The Program Manager window appears.

☛ Click on **File** in the menu bar. The **File** menu opens.

☛ Select **New**. The New Program Object dialog box appears.

☛ Select Program **G**roup and press **Enter**. The Program Group Properties dialog box appears.

☛ Type a title for your program group window. (For example, type Wilma's Work Group.) Press **Enter**. An empty program group window appears with whatever you typed as the title.

☛ Open the other program group windows and drag any icons you commonly use into your new program group window. (You may have to resize and rearrange windows to do this.)

☛ Click anywhere inside your new program group window to activate it.

☛ Open the **Windows** menu and select **Arrange Icons**. Windows automatically arranges the icons in your program group window so they don't overlap.

The Least You Need to Know

Microsoft Windows comes with a book that's over 600 pages long, so there's a lot more that you can know about Windows. However, here's some basic information you need to get started:

☛ To start Windows, change to the Windows directory (usually C:\WINDOWS), type **win**, and press **Enter**.

☛ To quit Windows, double-click on the Program Manager's control menu box.

☛ To run a program in Windows, change to the program group window that contains the program's icon and then double-click on the program's icon.

continues

continued

☞ To open a pull-down menu, click on the name of the menu in the menu bar.

☞ To select a command from a menu, click on the command.

☞ The buttons in the upper right corner of a window allow you to maximize, minimize, or restore the window to its original size.

☞ You can bring a window to the top of the stack by clicking on any portion of the window.

☞ You can resize a window by dragging one of the window's borders.

Part Two

Making Your Computer Do Something Useful

You may not even care about all the gadgets and gizmos that make up your computer. Chances are that when you type a letter, figure your taxes, or chase lemmings, you don't even notice your computer. You probably don't even notice DOS. The "hows" and "whys" of computing don't matter much when you've got to get something done.

This section talks about the "whats" that you're more interested in—what kinds of things you can do with a computer, what results you can expect, and what kinds of software and features you should use.

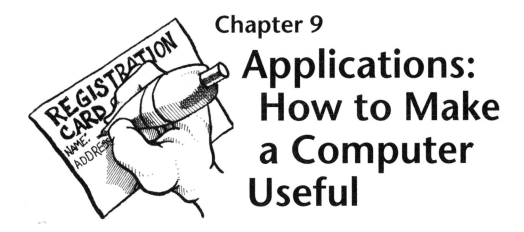

Chapter 9

Applications: How to Make a Computer Useful

In This Chapter

- ☛ What applications are and what they do
- ☛ Types of applications and what each type can do
- ☛ Figuring out whether your computer can run the application
- ☛ What to do when you get a new application
- ☛ Making a backup copy of your application disks
- ☛ Installing an application on your hard disk
- ☛ Running an application
- ☛ Common tasks you will perform in most applications

Without an operating system and an application program, your computer is about as useful as an overgrown paperweight. With just an operating system, your computer is an overgrown paperweight with eyes. For your

Before you get too far into the chapter, you should understand the terms "software," "program," and "application." *Software* consists of any instructions that tell your computer (the hardware) what to do. A *program* is a complete set of instructions (it is basically the same as software). A program can be an operating system (such as DOS) or an application. An *application* is a program that allows you to do something useful, such as type a letter or chase lemmings.

computer to become a useful member of society, it must be running an application program, a program that lets you do all sorts of fun and useful things like create newsletters, play games, and even get up-to-the-minute sports scores.

This chapter fills you in on the basics of application programs, including how to install programs on a hard disk and how to run programs.

The Right Application for the Right Job

As Table 9.1 shows, there's an application that can help you do just about any job you can think of. In later chapters, I will go into more detail about each type of application.

Table 9.1   Types of Applications

Application type	What you might want to use it for
Word processor	Writing letters and reports, composing books, writing articles.
Database	Storing and manipulating information, analyzing data, generating client reports, printing mailing labels.
Spreadsheet	Balancing accounts, keeping track of schedules, tracking materials, estimating job costs, determining averages, automating quality control.
Desktop publishing	Creating and printing newsletters, flyers, brochures, business cards, and books.
Telecommunications	Transferring data between two computers, accessing on-line information.
Graphics	Creating graphs, illustrating manuals, designing machinery.

Application type	What you might want to use it for
Integrated	Performing combined tasks of word processor, spreadsheet, database, communications, and graphics programs.
Utilities	Enhancing the capabilities of your computer, maintaining your computer and files, making your system easier to use.
Finance/Accounting	Printing checks, balancing a checkbook, managing payroll, updating inventory records.
Calendars	Keeping track of meetings and appointments.
Educational	Playing games (both educational and otherwise), composing music, researching topics.

How to Buy Software Your Computer Can Run

If you have a VHS tape player, you can't run Beta tapes on it. The same is true with a computer. You can't run all programs on all computers. Before you buy any application, make sure your computer can run it. The minimum hardware requirements are printed on the outside of every software package.

These hardware requirements will tell you whether you can run the program on an IBM-compatible computer, what type of microprocessor you need (286, 386, etc.), how much memory your computer needs, what version of DOS you need, whether Windows is required, whether you need a mouse, and so on. Make sure you have the equipment you need to run the program; otherwise, don't buy it.

A common thing to overlook when buying a program is the size of the disks the program comes on. If your computer has a 5 1/4-inch disk drive and the program comes on 3 1/2-inch disks, you won't be able to use the program. Some programs come with two sets of disks or with a coupon that lets you send in for the type of disks you need.

Disk Space: There's Never Enough

Not too long ago, the average program ate up only a few megabytes of hard disk space. Nowadays, a fancy program can gobble up 15 megabytes of space and still be hungry for more.

Before you buy a program, make sure your disk has enough room for it. Change to the disk drive you want to check. Type **dir** and press **Enter**. DOS displays a list of files in the current drive and directory. At the bottom of the list is the amount of disk space.

DOS displays the amount of disk space in bytes. To convert bytes to megabytes, add commas to the number. For example, if DOS says there are 40456798 bytes, add commas to make the number look like this: 40,456,798. The disk has 40 million bytes—about 40 megabytes.

By the Way . . .

A hard disk is a lot like a house; it seems big until you move in. When looking at the amount of disk space, make sure you look at the Free Space not the Total Space. Half your disk space may already be occupied.

Does Your Computer Have the Necessary Brainpower?

In addition to being disk hogs, many programs are memory hogs, requiring 2 to 4 megabytes of memory before they'll even say hello. Does your computer have enough memory to run the program? To find out, type **mem** at the DOS prompt and press **Enter**. DOS displays the amount of memory installed in your computer.

What You Should Find in the Software Box

When you get your software package home, open the box and spread everything out on a table. Make sure you got everything you paid for.

You should find the *disks* that contain the program files, an *instruction manual* explaining how to use the program, and a *registration card.*

Register Your Software

As soon as you open the software package, you'll be tempted to fling the registration card in the trash. I know it's hard, but try to resist the temptation. Complete the registration card and mail it back to the manufacturer. Why? Because the card lets the manufacturer know who owns a legal copy of the program. Most software manufacturers offer perks for returning the card. They may answer your questions over the phone, offer program upgrades (newer versions of the program) at greatly reduced prices, and give your name to every junk mail joint in the country.

Protect Your Investment: Write-Protect the Disks

TECHNO NERD TEACHES

There are three basic types of memory: *conventional, extended,* and *expanded.* Conventional memory is what most programs use; it is the first 640 kilobytes of memory. You can add memory to your computer in the form of extended or expanded memory. (You add extended memory by installing additional RAM chips. You add expanded memory by installing an expanded memory board.) This memory requires special software called a *memory manager* for programs to use it. Windows comes with a memory manager that allows Windows programs to use extended memory.

Now you're ready to start using the program. Stop. You're not ready. Before you begin using the floppy disks included in the software package, protect the disks from damage by write-protecting them. *Write-protection* lets your computer read the disk files but not change any information on the disk. It's sort of like breaking the tab off the back of a VHS tape so you won't record over your favorite movie.

To write-protect a 5 1/4-inch disk, cover the write-protect notch with a write-protect sticker. The 3 1/2-inch disks have a sliding write-protect tab. To write-protect these disks, slide the tab so that you can see through the window. (Many manufacturers write-protect the disks for you, but don't count on it.)

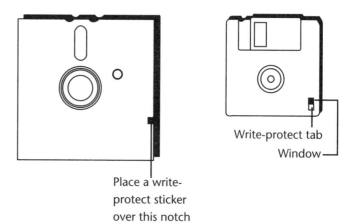

Write-protect your program disks to protect the files they contain.

Place a write-protect sticker over this notch

Write-protect tab

Window

Better Than the Real Thing: Using Working Copies

Unless you like to tempt fate and pay for everything twice, you should never use the original program disks for performing your daily tasks. Always make copies of the original disks and then use the copies to install or use the program. Store the original disks in a safe place, so you'll have them in case the copies get damaged. Read on to learn how to make working copies.

By the Way . . .

I put all this stuff about copying disks in here, because it's the standard, overly safe way of doing things. If the original disks are write-protected and you plan to install the program on a hard disk, don't waste your time creating backup copies. When you install the program on your hard disk, that will be your working copy, and the originals will be your backups. Skip all this drivel and go to the section called "Getting the Program Up and Running."

Get Some Blank Disks

To copy disks, first obtain a set of blank disks that are the same *size* and *density* as the program disks you want to copy. You cannot copy low-density disks to high-density disks or vice versa. Don't worry about formatting the disks; DOS formats the disks during the copy operation.

Copying Disks with DOS

Once you have the blank disks, making copies is easy (but not very interesting).

Start by typing **diskcopy a: a:** (or **diskcopy b: b:**) and pressing **Enter**. Insert the original program disk into the drive you specified (a: or b:), and close the drive door, if it has a door. Press any key. DOS reads the information from the disk and stores it in memory.

If you have two floppy disk drives of the same size and capacity, you can use both drives to speed up the disk copying. Insert the original program disk into drive A and the blank disk into drive B. Type **diskcopy a: b:** and press **Enter**.

When DOS prompts you, insert one of the blank disks in the specified drive and press any key. DOS writes the information stored in memory onto the blank disk. Follow the on-screen messages until you've created a copy of each program disk.

If you type the DISKCOPY command and get a message that says **Bad command or filename**, change to the DOS directory (type **cd \dos** and press **Enter**) and enter the command again.

What's Wrong with This Picture?

You get a new program, and you don't want your brand-new disks to get damaged, so you decide to copy the disks. You get a set of blank disks, and you use the DISKCOPY command to create working copies of the original disks.

Answer: You forgot to write-protect the original disks. If, during the disk copy operation, you get the original and blank disks mixed up, you might end up copying the blank disk to the original. (I've done this once myself.) By write-protecting the original disks, you can prevent such a catastrophe.

Getting the Program Up and Running

Before you can use a program, you usually have to perform two preliminary steps: *installing* the program (if you have a hard disk) and *running* it.

Filling Up Your Hard Disk the Easy Way: Installing a Program

If a program requires a hard disk, you must install the program before you can run it. Although "installing a program" sounds about as complicated as installing central air conditioning, it's more like installing a toaster (plugging it in). Most programs come with an installation program (called setup or install) that does everything for you. You just relax, eat donuts, and swap disks in and out of a drive.

> ### By the Way . . .
> Because the installation procedure varies from program to program, you should consult the instructions that came with the program to determine the correct procedure. If you don't have the instructions, refer to Chapter 19, "Surviving Without Documentation" to figure out what to do.

Running a Program: Play It Again, Sam

Chapters 7 and 8 explain how to run programs from the DOS prompt or in Windows. But since you probably skipped the first section to get to the juicy stuff here in section 2, here's a brief review.

To run a DOS program, change to the drive and directory that contains the program files, type the command for running the program, and press **Enter**. To run a Windows program, display the program group window that contains the program's icon, and then double-click on the icon.

> **By the Way . . .**
> If you can't remember the command for running the program, skip ahead to Chapter 19 to learn how to fake your way into the program.

Meeting Your Program for the First Time

After you run (start) the program, it may take a while for the computer to read the program from disk and load it into RAM. How fast the program loads depends on the speed of your computer and the complexity of the program. When the program is loaded, you'll see a main menu, a pull-down menu bar, or a blank work area. In any case, this is the screen on which you will start working.

Application Rites and Rituals

Most programs act as though you have to know everything about the program before you begin. That's baloney. If you can figure out how to do three things in any program, you have a pretty good start. What three things? How to save, open, and print a file.

The first thing you should learn how to do in a program is create or save a file. This ensures that any work you do is permanently saved to disk. To save a file, you usually enter the Save command and then type a name for the file. The program does the rest, saving the file to disk. Once you save the file for the first time, you never have to name it again. The next time you want to save the file, you simply enter the Save command.

Once the file is saved, you can open it at any time and continue working on it. Opening a file generally consists of entering the Open command and then telling the program the location and name of the file you want to open.

If you want a paper copy of the file, you'll have to know how to print the file. This is pretty easy once you've set up the program to recognize your printer. You simply enter the Print command, provide the program with some print instructions (print quality, number of copies, and so on), and unleash the program. It takes care of the rest.

Help! Finding Your Way Out of Software Oblivion

When you're using a program and you get in a jam, you can often get the help you need by staring at the screen. Many programs contain message bars that provide information about the task you're trying to perform. If there's no message or if the message doesn't help, you can get more information by accessing the program's help system.

When in doubt, try pressing the **F1** key. Many programs use this key to display context-sensitive help. With a good context-sensitive help system, you can usually get by without the documentation. But don't tell anyone I said so.

Most programs offer two forms of help: context-sensitive help and a help index. *Context-sensitive help* provides information about the screen you're currently working on. The program knows the task you're trying to perform; when you ask for Help, the program offers the information it thinks you need. A *help index*, on the other hand, lets you choose a help topic from a list of topics.

The Least You Need to Know

So much for application basic training. Try to remember these survival skills for your future forays into the application jungle.

- ☛ Not all computers can run all programs. Before buying a program, make sure your computer can run it.

- ☛ When you first get a program, complete the registration card and mail it to the manufacturer.

- ☛ Before using the program disks, copy them and use the copies to install or run the program.

- ☛ Most programs come with an installation program that installs the program for you. This program creates the required directory on the hard disk, and copies the program files to the directory. The installation program may also uncompress the files if they are in a compressed format.

- ☛ To run a DOS program, type the command required to start the program and then press **Enter**.

- ☛ To run a Windows program, double-click on the program's icon.

- ☛ Most applications allow you to perform the following basic tasks: create a file, save a file, open a file, print a file, and quit the program.

- ☛ Many applications come with a context-sensitive help system that provides information for the task you are currently trying to perform. (When in doubt, try pressing **F1** for help.)

Chapter 10

Processing Words and Other Vegetables

In This Chapter

- What a word-processing program is
- The four basic steps in creating a document
- What to expect when you start typing
- Saving your work to disk
- Opening a file
- Editing your work
- Moving around inside a document
- Advanced word-processing features

Whoever came up with the idea of calling a program that lets you type letters in a word-processing program?

"What are you doing, honey?"

"Oh, just processing a few words."

. . . sort of like shredding carrots and purple cabbage for a salad.

So what is a word-processing program? It's a program that essentially transforms your computer into a fancy typewriter that not only makes typing a lot easier, but can actually help you compose and perfect your work. It has an endless supply of electronic "paper" that scrolls past the screen as you type, and because it's electronic, you don't have to worry about making mistakes. Just go back and type over the errors—no messy correction fluid, no erasing, and best of all, no retyping.

A Bird's Eye View of Word Processing

Most word-processing programs that are worth their salt come with a lot of fancy features that let you do somersaults with text and pictures. Many users spend a good part of their adult lives learning how to use these features to improve their work and save time. However, if you just want to type and print a simple document like a letter, you need to know how to perform only a few simple tasks:

Type You need to type the first draft of whatever you're working on.

Edit Once you have something to work with, you can experiment with the information on-screen until it is just the way you want it.

Format At any time, you can begin working on the appearance of the document. This includes setting margins and line spacing, setting tabs, changing the way the text is aligned, and changing typestyles.

Print You can print the document when it's complete or at any time during its creation.

Typing on Electronic Paper

Most word-processing programs start out with a blank "sheet of paper" on-screen. The screen is about a third as long as a real sheet of paper, and it may be black instead of white, so you'll have to use your imagination. The program also displays a *cursor* or *insertion point*; anything you type will be inserted at this point.

When the cursor reaches the bottom of the screen, the program will move the "page" up, so you can continue typing. This is called *scrolling*.

Most programs display a horizontal line across the screen to show where each page will end in print.

Easing the Transition

People who move from a typewriter to a computer commonly run into the same problems. To ease you through the transition from paper to computer, I'll give you some free advice.

First, press Enter only to end a paragraph. With a word-processing program, you don't press Enter or Return at the end of every line. The program automatically *wraps* text from one line to the next as you type. Press Enter or Return only to end a paragraph or to break a line.

As you type, remember that any text that won't fit on the screen scrolls off the top of the screen. Just because something doesn't appear on-screen doesn't mean it is gone. If you type more than a screenful of text, any text that does not fit in the screen is *scrolled* off the top of the screen. You can see the text by pressing PgUp or using the up arrow key to move the cursor to the top of the document.

Once you have text on-screen, use only the arrow keys or the mouse to move the cursor. Many people try to move the cursor down by pressing the Enter key. This starts a new paragraph. Worse, some people try to move the cursor left by pressing the Backspace key. This moves the cursor alright, but it deletes any characters in the cursor's path. To move the cursor safely, use the arrow keys.

To delete any characters, you can use the Delete or Backspace key. To delete a character that the cursor is on or a character to the right of the cursor, press the **Del** (Delete) key. To delete characters to the left of the cursor, press the **Backspace** key. Just remember, "Delete to the right; Backspace to the left."

Just Do It

Once you've grasped the behavior of word-processing programs, typing is easy—just do it. In a word-processing program, text is like clay. You can add text anywhere, delete text, and even lop off a paragraph or two and slap them somewhere else in the document. The next few sections explain some of the word-processing tools and techniques you can use to move around in a document and enter your changes.

Zipping Around Inside a Document

When you're in a document, it's like being in a crowded city. You have all these little characters on-screen elbowing each other for a little breathing room. You are the cursor—the little on-screen light—and you can weave your way through the crowds. The *arrow keys* let you move the cursor up, down, left, or right one character at a time.

To move faster (one word at a time), most programs let you use the *Ctrl* (Control) key along with the arrow keys. You hold down the Ctrl key while pressing the arrow key to leap from one word to the next.

To move at warp speed, you can use the *Home* and *End* keys. The Home key usually moves the cursor to the beginning of a line. End moves the cursor to the end of a line.

What about the text that scrolled off the screen? Use the *PgUp* key to move up one screen at a time, or *PgDn* to move down one screen at a time. Remember, a screen is shorter than an actual page.

Most programs have additional key combinations for moving the cursor to the top or bottom of a document, from paragraph to paragraph, or from sentence to sentence, but these keys vary widely from program to program.

To Insert or To Overstrike?

In most programs, if you move the cursor between two words or two characters and start typing, whatever you type is inserted at the cursor. Any surrounding text gets bumped to the right to make room for the new kids. This is known as *Insert mode*, and it is the mode that most programs function in (unless you specify otherwise).

You can switch modes to *Overstrike mode* in order to type over what's already on-screen. If you want to replace one word with another, you simply type over the word you want to delete. In most programs, you can switch back and forth between Insert and Overstrike modes by pressing the Ins key.

When a program starts in a certain mode, that mode is referred to as the *default mode*. Because nothing was specified, the program defaults to a particular setting, usually the safest or most common setting.

Rubbing Out Undesirable Characters

The simplest way to delete characters on-screen is to move the cursor to the character you want to delete and press **Del** (Delete). This key works a little differently from program to program—sometimes the cursor deletes the character it's on; other times it deletes the character to the right. In either case, you'll get used to it pretty quickly.

Making Room for the New Text on the Block

As you type corrections, add or delete words, and insert phrases into your document, you'll notice that you don't have to worry about adjusting the surrounding text to accommodate the change. The word-processing program does it automatically, rewrapping the words in a paragraph to compensate for whatever change you enter.

Computerized Scissors and Tape

Usually, revising a document is not a simple matter of changing a word here or there or correcting typos. You may need to delete an entire sentence or even rearrange the paragraphs to present your ideas in a more logical flow. To help you get it done, most word-processing programs offer *block commands*.

Using these commands is a simple two-step process. First, mark or select the area of text (the block) you want to work with. The block you select appears highlighted.

When you start seeing how much you can do with block commands, you may worry that you can do an equal amount of damage to your document. For minor mistakes, such as deleting a line or a paragraph, most programs have a safety buffer, much like the holding area described earlier. If you unintentionally erase some text, you can usually get it back by entering an "Undo" command. (If your program has pull-down menus, check the Edit menu for this command.) Keep in mind, however, that the buffer remembers only a limited number of changes (usually one).

The second step consists of cutting or copying the block to a temporary holding area called the *Clipboard*. The *Cut* command removes the marked block from the document. *Copy* places a clone of the marked block on the Clipboard, leaving the original alone. In either case, you can *paste* the block from the Clipboard into another location in the document or into another document.

Find a Needle in a Haystack? No Problem

Say you write a company training manual that explains how to make a three-legged chair. After testing reveals that people fall over less frequently in more expensive four-legged chairs and (understandably) prefer their stability, the company decides to manufacture four-legged chairs instead of three-legged chairs. You can use the search and replace feature to replace all occurrences of *three-legged chair* with *four-legged chair*. (Most word-processing programs have a separate Search command, which searches for specified text without replacing the text.)

Many spell-checkers have *dictionaries* and boast the number of words included. Don't expect these dictionaries to function as *Webster's Ninth*. The dictionaries are used by the spell-checking feature to determine correct spellings; most of these dictionaries don't contain definitions.

An On-Screen Proofreader

It's always good to have another set of eyes look over a letter or manuscript before you send it out. Many word-processing programs include a spell-checker that can check your document for spelling errors, typos, repeated words (such as "the the"), and incorrect capitalization (tHe). (These spell-checkers cannot, however, spot mistyped words; for example, if you typed "two" instead of "too" or "its" instead of "it's.")

It's Right on the Tip of My Tongue

If you can't think of the right word, press a button to open the thesaurus. Enter the best word you can come up with, and your word-processing program will display a list of synonyms (words that have the same or similar meaning). You simply select a word from the list.

Grammar Checkers: No, It's Not a Game You Play with Your Grandma

If you think grammar is a nice old lady who used to give you cookies and milk, you probably need a grammar checker. A grammar checker can scan your documents for common grammatical errors, including overuse of the passive voice, subject/verb disagreement, wordy sentences, overly long sentences, incomplete sentences, and more.

In addition, most grammar checkers provide an overall rating for a document to show whether the document is suitable for the intended audience. For example, if you're writing a memo to somebody in management, you should probably shoot above a third grade reading level. The grammar checker will analyze the complexity and length of the words you used and the complexity and length of the sentences. It will then let you know whether your work is overly complex (you might have to use more pictures).

OOPS!

Although more and more word-processing programs are coming equipped with their own grammar checkers, you might have to buy a separate program. Just make sure that the grammar checker you get can work with the files you create in your word-processing program. Try Grammatik or Right Writer.

Making Your Document Look Pretty

Once you have the content of your document under control and you've fixed all your typos and misspellings, you can start working on the appearance of your document—how you want it to look on paper. This is called *formatting* the document. You will basically format two aspects of the document: the overall page and line layout and the look of the characters.

Page and Line Formatting

Here are some of the overall formatting options that most word-processing programs offer. (Your program's help system or documentation can give you even more information about these options.)

A *widow* is the last line of a paragraph that appears alone at the top of the next page. If the first line of the paragraph gets stranded at the bottom of a page, it is called an *orphan*. Just remember that an orphan is left behind.

☞ Set left/right margins

☞ Number pages

☞ Align the text

☞ Center a word, line, or block of text

☞ Adjust the line spacing

☞ Set page length

☞ Set top/bottom margins

☞ Create headers and footers

☞ Prevent widows and orphans

More Character for Characters

To emphasize key words and phrases, many word-processing programs let you select from various fonts and typestyles. In other words, you can make the letters look big and fancy, as in a magazine, or small and hard to read, like the fine print on a loan.

A *font* is any set of characters of the same *typeface* (design) and *typesize* (measured in points). For example, Helvetica 12-point is a font; Helvetica is the typeface, and 12-point is the size. (Just for reference, there are 72 points in an inch.) A *typestyle* is any variation that enhances the existing font. For example, boldface, italics, and underlining are all typestyles; the character's design and size stay the same, but an aspect of the type is changed.

Be Safe: Save Your Work

Listen, Charles Keating is not in your computer, so don't be afraid to save your work to disk. Only by saving your work to disk will it be safe. It's usually as simple as pulling down the File menu and selecting Save.

The Unveiling: Seeing It in Print

You've done all the hard work—the writing, editing, formatting, and reformatting. All you need to do now is print your final creation to have all those electronic characters transformed into a real document.

Printing your document essentially consists of telling the computer to send the file to your printer. The printer uses the information from the file to determine what characters to print, and then prints those characters on paper.

If you're shopping for software that includes special typestyles and fonts, make sure your printer can keep up. Although most printers can handle one or two typestyles (boldface and underline), many printers cannot handle various fonts.

If your word-processing program has a pull-down menu bar, the Print command is usually on the File menu.

Author's Pick: Best Word-Processing Program

I talk about several of my favorite programs in Chapter 22, but I'll give you a little preview by telling you about my favorite word-processing programs here.

First, if it were my dollar, I'd go for a Microsoft Windows word processor: Microsoft Word 2 for Windows or Ami Pro. These programs offer full-time WYSIWYG (What-You-See-Is-What-You-Get), so you can see exactly what the text, art, and everything else will look like on-screen before you print it. These programs also allow you to paste text and art on the same page (just as you might do in a desktop publishing program).

If you don't have Windows, go with WordPerfect for DOS. You can do everything you would ever want to do with a word processor using this program: combine text and graphics, add simple vertical and horizontal lines to a page, create columns of text like you see in a newspaper, and more. Trouble is, it's not as easy to do all these things as it is to do them in a Windows word processor.

For some less expensive word-processing programs, try Professional Write or LetterPerfect (a scaled-down version of WordPerfect).

The Least You Need to Know

As you get more experienced with a word-processing program, you will naturally start to use the more advanced features. When you are just starting out, however, stick to these basics:

☞ When you start a word-processing program, you get a blank screen with a cursor or insertion point. Anything you type is inserted at the cursor.

☞ Word processors let you create documents in four simple steps: type the document, edit it, format it, and print the final product.

☞ To move around in a document, use the arrow keys, the PgUp key, the PgDn key, and the mouse.

☞ Block commands let you move, copy, delete a block of text, or change the line spacing or font of an entire block.

☞ Most word processors let you undo a deletion.

☞ Page formatting lets you position your document on the page, number the pages, print on different page sizes, add headers or footers, and prevent widows and orphans.

☞ You can format characters to set off words, phrases, headings, or even entire sections of text.

☞ Save and Print commands let you store electronic versions and create paper versions of your documents. If your program has pull-down menus, look for these commands on the File menu.

Chapter 11

Getting to First Base with a Database

In This Chapter

- What a database is and what it can do for you
- Creating a form for gathering data
- Typing information into a database using your form
- Using a database to sort records
- Finding records at the touch of a key
- Creating lists and mailing labels
- Pulling information out of the database to create reports

You probably come in contact with databases every day of your life without ever realizing it. For example, say you walk into a bookstore and ask the clerk if they have a copy of *Confidence Man*. The clerk goes over to the computer, types something, and then says, "Yes, it's in Fiction, under Melville." The clerk used a database to quickly look up the information.

In this chapter, you'll learn how such a database works and how you can create a database to manage your own information.

> ## By the Way . . .
> You don't have to create a database in order to use one. I have a database called *Banner Blue Movie Guide,* which contains information about 9,000 movies. This program lets me look up movies by title, actor, and director. However, if you have information that you want to manage using a database, you will have to create your own database.

The Making of a Database: A Quick Overview

Before you get mired in all the gory details of what it takes to create a database, look at the overall process. It consists of two basic steps: you create a blank *form* and then type information on the form to create *records.* Okay, it's a little more complicated than that, but not much.

Creating a Form for Gathering Information

Forms simulate, on the computer screen, the paper forms you fill out with a pen or pencil, such as an insurance claim, a tax return, or a Rolodex card.

A *record* is a collection of information about a single topic; it may contain the specifications for a gear or the name, address, and accounting information for a client. A collection of these records makes up a database.

To create a form, you must enter *field names* to indicate where each piece of information should be typed. These names are equivalent to what you see on paper forms: Last Name, First Name, MI, SSN, and so on.

It's as Simple as Filling in the Blanks

Once you have a form, you can fill in the blanks with information (or put an ad in the paper for a data-entry operator). The blanks in this case are referred to as *fields.* By entering information into the fields, you create a *record*, as shown in this picture. A database file is a collection of records.

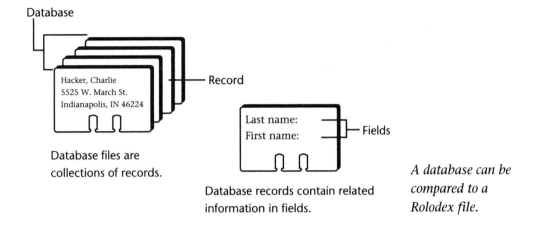

Database

Hacker, Charlie
5525 W. March St.
Indianapolis, IN 46224

Record

Database files are
collections of records.

Last name:
First name:

Fields

Database records contain related
information in fields.

*A database can be
compared to a
Rolodex file.*

Forming the Perfect Form

Designing the form requires a great deal of foresight. You must anticipate what information you will need, approximately how long the maximum entry in each field will be, what kind of information will be entered in each field (characters or numbers), and what is the clearest, most concise wording for your field names.

The best way to start designing a form is to follow the non-computer system you're presently using—your Rolodex, phone book, calendar, list of employees, accounts receivable, inventory list, or whatever. Think up field names for each piece of information you'll need. Weed out any unnecessary information—you don't want to turn your database into a junkyard.

When you're typing field names, you may want to press your Caps Lock key to type the names in all uppercase letters. That way, you can easily see where the field name ends and the field entry begins.

> ### By the Way . . .
> When you're designing the form, be sure to break the information into small units so you can pull small bits of information out of the database later. For example, if you need to record a name, create a separate field for the person's title (Mr./Ms./Mrs.), first name, last name, and middle initial. By doing this, you will be able to pull out each piece of information separately (for example, you will be able to pull only the person's last name). This is useful for creating form letters addressed to various individuals.

What's Wrong with This Picture?

Point out some of the problems with the following form:

Name
Birthday:
Social Security Number:
Address:
Phone number:

Answers:

Name field   The Name field does not break the name out into last name, first name, middle initial, and title. You might want to pull out a person's first name separately later, for example in a greeting such as "Dear Bill."

Social Security Number field   The field name is longer than it needs to be; abbreviate it SSN.

Address field   The address should be broken out into Street Address, City, State, and ZIP.

Phone Number field   There should be an example to show how to enter the phone number—for example, (NNN)NNN-NNNN.

Saving the Blank Form

When you're done creating the fields for your form, you usually save the form or choose a command for entering data. In either case, the database program will display the form you created. The field names appear, showing you the information you must enter.

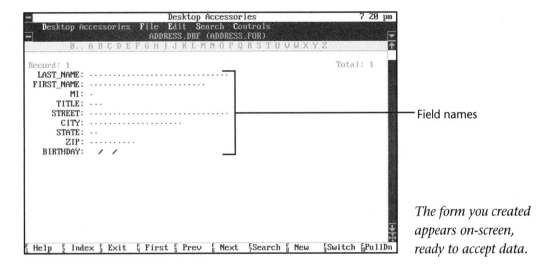

Field names

The form you created appears on-screen, ready to accept data.

Filling Out Forms, Forms, and More Forms

When you start filling out your forms, you'll feel like you're spending eternity in a doctor's office. Here's where you enter all the information that you want to include in the database—names, addresses, company contacts, part numbers, prices, and inventory lists.

To move from one field to the next on a form, you usually press **Tab**. To move back one field, press **Shift+Tab**. If the program offers mouse support, you can move to a field by clicking on it.

OOPS!

Make sure the form is just as you want it before you start entering information into the fields for the form. Some programs offer a way for you to edit field names later and reorient your database, but even in these cases you need to be careful.

In some databases, you can get the database to automatically format your entries. For example, the program may add dollar signs, decimals, and commas to show dollar values. In such a case, remember not to type these symbols when entering your data.

Be sure to check the entries on-screen against your source. It's pretty easy to edit field entries later, but if you enter Jehnson when you meant to enter Johnson and you try to find Johnson's record later, your database won't know what you're looking for.

Some database programs, like Paradox, save records automatically. This is a nice feature that makes it almost impossible to lose your data.

Save Each Record Separately

Once you've entered all the information you have for a record, save the record. This usually consists of selecting a single command as indicated on your screen. The program saves the information you entered and displays a blank form, ready for you to enter information for the next record.

Entering Additional Records

You may need to enter a command to display the next blank form. Your database program's documentation or help system can tell you how. Continue filling out forms until all the information you need in your database is entered.

Ferreting Out Information in the Database

Now that you have this oversized filing cabinet sitting in your computer, how do you go about getting at those records? You have at least three options:

☞ Browse through the records one at a time.

☞ List the information in every record according to field name.

☞ Search for a specific record or range of records.

Just Browsing, Thanks

Browsing consists of flipping through the electronic pages of your database. Browsing is fairly slow and is useful only for finding a record when you don't know what record you want to find. If you have even a vague notion of which record you need, you're better off using one of the other two methods.

Gimme the List

Instead of displaying each record on a single screen, the list option displays each record on a single line (from left to right across the screen). Although some of the information for each record will be off the right of the screen, you will be able to see a small portion of each record.

In Search of a Single Record

Searching for a single record is the fastest and easiest way to find a specific record or group of records. If you enter a command telling the database to search, it responds by asking what you want to search for.

In most databases, you must specify the field in which you want to search and the information you want to find in that field. The entry you type is referred to as *search criteria*. For example, if you want to find out how many paddles your sales representative Alan sold in the month of March, you would have to instruct the database to search the Month field for March, search the Name field for Alan, and display the number in the Paddles field.

Searching for a Range of Records

In addition to searching for an individual record, you can tell the database to search for a group of records. For example, to search for purchase order numbers 10013 to 10078, or companies with outstanding invoices of $300 to $1,500, you can enter the specific range in the field you want to search.

When You Don't Know What You're Looking For

After you've entered a hundred or a thousand records, no one can seriously expect you to remember the exact spelling of every entry in every field. You'll forget a few, and you need some way of finding these records. That's why most database programs let you use *wild cards* to search for records. (Wild cards stand in for particular characters you can't remember.)

Get Organized!

As you enter records into your database, the database stores the records in the order that you enter them. If you entered a stack of records in no particular order, your database is a mess. If you call up a list of records, they appear in no logical order. Luckily, the database can sort your records in whatever order you specify and present you with a neat, orderly stack.

Put It to Work

Just look at the practical things you can do with the sort feature:

Sales analysis   Sort the records for your sales force to determine who's selling the most goods and making you the most profit.

Ranking   Rank students by grades to determine the most effective mix for group activities.

Follow-ups   Sort invoices by date past due, so you can find out who has owed you money for the longest time. Sort by total amount due to find out who owes you the most money.

Bulk rates   Print out form letters grouped by ZIP code to take advantage of bulk rates.

Rosters   Print out a list of employees or a list of clients by phone number to create telemarketing lists. Find out which clients haven't placed an order recently to determine who you should call first.

Telling the Database How to Sort

Like the search feature, the sort feature requires you to enter criteria in whatever field you want to sort. For example, if you want to sort your records by last name, you might type 1 in the LAST NAME field or enter a command, such as

SORT ON LAST_NAME TO ALPHA

telling the program to sort the records according to the entry in the LAST NAME field and store the index in a file called ALPHA.DBF.

Breaking the Tie

Because some records may contain the same entry in the field you choose to sort, many programs let you enter sort criteria in more than one field. The criteria entered in the first field is called the *primary sort criteria*, and the criteria entered in the second field is referred to as the *secondary sort criteria*. If there's a tie in the primary field, the database looks to the entry in the secondary field to determine how to sort the records.

A to Z or Z to A?

When you're entering sort criteria, you can specify whether you want the records sorted in *ascending* order (A, B, C...1, 2, 3) or *descending* order (Z, Y, X...10, 9, 8), and whether you want them sorted alphabetically or by number. Otherwise, the program sorts the records according to its default setting (usually alphabetical ascending order).

Creating Form Letters, Reports, and Mailing Labels

You've seen how much power the field names give you in searching and sorting your records, but that's not the half of it. You can also use the field names to yank information out of your records and to consolidate it in a single location.

For example, you can merge the database with a form letter to create a series of letters all addressed to different people. In the letter, you would use field names to indicate where you want information from the database to be inserted. You would then *merge* your letter with your database. The merge process would look up information in your database and insert it in the form letter, creating a separate letter for each selected record in the database.

You can also use the merge feature to create reports or invoices. Set up a sheet with several column headings that correspond to the field names in your database. Merge the sheet with your database to create a comprehensive report or invoice containing all of the information you need.

To create mailing labels, create a single mailing label consisting of field names in the place of actual names and addresses. Merge the label with your database to print an entire roll of mailing labels in a matter of minutes.

Choosing the Right Database for You

Database programs vary in how they structure the database and in the special features they offer. That's not to say that one is better than the other. You just need to find the one that's right for your needs and budget. You can choose from among three types of databases: free-form, flat-file, and relational.

A *free-form database* mimics the random pile of notes you might find cluttered on a desk. When you search for data, the program searches the entire database—not just a specified field. Popular free-form databases include MemoryMate and Info Select.

A *flat-file database* works like a Rolodex. Each record in the file contains the same type of information entered in standard fields, such as names, addresses, and telephone numbers. Popular flat-file databases include Q&A, FileMaker Pro, PC-File, and Reflex.

A *relational database* is the most powerful type of database because it can use two or more database files and combine them into a new, separate file. For example, you can create one database for inventory and another for invoices. Whenever you create an invoice that charges a customer for an inventory item, the inventory database is updated to show that the item was removed. Popular relational databases include dBASE IV, FoxPro, Oracle, Paradox, and Fourth Dimension.

By the Way . . .

You may have a database and not know it. Many non-database programs contain a primitive database program or a way to create a database. For example, a word-processing program may allow you to type names and addresses into a document file and use it for a database. Spreadsheet programs, including Excel and Quattro Pro for Windows, allow you to create databases using the basic spreadsheet structure. So, don't go out and buy an expensive database program if you don't need one.

The Least You Need to Know

Although a database can be a complicated tool to master, you don't need to know very much to get started. To sort it all out, keep the following information in mind:

- ☞ A database consists of several records containing field entries.

- ☞ To create a database, you create a form and then fill out the form to create records.

- ☞ When you save a record, you're storing information in your database.

- ☞ You can search your database by browsing page by page, by displaying a list of records, or by entering search criteria for a specific record or range of records.

continues

continued

☞ To sort your records, you must enter sort criteria, telling your database which fields to use for sorting and whether to sort in ascending or descending order.

☞ Field names give you the power to pull information from your database and insert it into a document. This lets you generate comprehensive reports, personalized letters, and mailing labels.

☞ Free-form databases are best for storing random thoughts and data. Because they lack a structure, sorting and finding data can be difficult.

☞ Flat-file databases store structured information and can be easy to use, but cannot combine data from two or more files.

☞ Relational databases are the most powerful, letting you share data among databases.

Chapter 12

Between the Sheets with Spreadsheets

In This Chapter

- Using a spreadsheet to do your math for you
- How to move around in a spreadsheet
- Adding formulas to a spreadsheet to perform calculations
- Using ready-made formulas for complex calculations
- Making a professional looking spreadsheet by adding lines and shading
- Some practical uses for spreadsheets
- Using the spreadsheet to play with numbers

There's no mystery to spreadsheets. A checkbook is a spreadsheet. A calendar is a spreadsheet. Your 1040 tax form is a spreadsheet. Any sheet that has boxes you can fill in is a type of spreadsheet.

So, what's so special about computerized spreadsheets? Computerized spreadsheets perform any required calculations for you. For example, a computerized checkbook spreadsheet can calculate your balance whenever you enter a transaction. You type the amount of the check, and the spreadsheet subtracts it from your balance. You enter a deposit, and the program adds the deposit to your balance.

In this chapter, you'll learn what it takes to create your own spreadsheets.

Taking the Spread Out of Spreadsheets

A spreadsheet is a sheet with a spread. What's a spread? It's a grid—a series of columns and rows that intersect to form thousands of small boxes called *cells*.

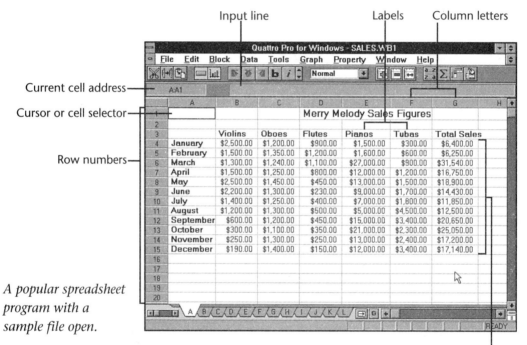

A popular spreadsheet program with a sample file open.

Formulas in these cells add the sales figures for each month.

A *cell* is a box formed by the intersection of a column and a row in a spreadsheet grid.

Columns, Rows, and Where They Cross

Look across the top of any computer spreadsheet, and you'll see the alphabet (A, B, C, and so on). Each letter stands at the head of a *column*. Along the left side of the spreadsheet, you'll see numbers representing *rows*. The place where a column and row intersect forms a box, called a *cell*. This is the basic unit of any spreadsheet. You will type text, values, and formulas in the cells to make your spreadsheet.

Knowing Where a Cell Lives

If a spreadsheet loses a cell, it's in deep Voodoo. To keep track of cells, the spreadsheet uses *cell addresses*. Each cell has an address that consists of a column letter and row number. For example, the cell that's formed by the intersection of column G and row 11 has the address G11. You can label the columns and rows with meaningful headings, so you don't have to guess what the letters mean.

Cell Hopping

Look in the upper left corner of the spreadsheet, and you'll see a shaded rectangle. This is the cursor; it allows you to leap from one cell to the next. The cursor fills an entire cell, and the contents of that cell are usually displayed in an *input bar* or *input line* at the top of the screen. To move the cursor, you can use a mouse to click on the desired cell, or you can use the arrow keys, the Tab key, and the PgUp and PgDn keys.

Some spreadsheet programs let you name individual cells or groups of cells (ranges). You can then use the names, rather than cell addresses, to refer to the cells.

Some programs offer scroll bars to help you move quickly to different areas of the spreadsheet using your mouse. To move one cell at a time, you click on an arrow at the end of the scroll bar to move in the direction of the arrow. To move faster, you can drag the scroll box in the direction you want to move.

Where Am I? The Status Bar

A spreadsheet is like a huge mega-mall; it's easy to get lost. You need one of those maps that has an arrow pointing and saying "You Are Here" in big bold letters. Well, you won't get that exactly, but most spreadsheets do display a status bar at the top of the screen that shows the address of the active cell. The status bar also shows the contents of the cell so that you can edit it if you want to.

Building a Spreadsheet from the Ground Up

Before you can use a spreadsheet to perform numbers magic, you have to create one. This process can be very, very simple or very, very complicated, depending on what you want the spreadsheet to do. However, the overall process is always the same.

First, you design the spreadsheet by thinking through what it should look like. Next, you label the columns and rows, and then enter the formulas and functions that the spreadsheet will use to perform calculations. At this point, you can also format the cells (to display dollar signs, for instance) to make entering data quick and easy.

After the basic spreadsheet setup is in place, you should perform a test run to make sure the spreadsheet works. Once you've eliminated any problems you identify during the test run, you can enter your data. Finally, you can finish up by saving and printing the spreadsheet.

By the Way . . .

There's no law that says you have to perform the steps in this order. Many users like to enter their data first and then perform the other steps. Regardless of how you proceed, you will probably have to go back to previous steps to fine-tune your spreadsheet.

Designing the Spreadsheet (Even If You Have No Fashion Sense)

If you have a form that you want the spreadsheet to look like, lay the form down by your keyboard and use it as a model. For example, if you're going to use the spreadsheet to balance your checkbook, use your most recent bank statement or your checkbook to set up the columns and rows.

If you don't have a form, draw your spreadsheet on a piece of paper or a napkin to determine the columns and rows you need. (It doesn't have to be perfect, just something to get started.)

What's In a Name?

When you have some idea of the basic structure of your spreadsheet and the tasks you want it to perform, you're ready to enter *labels*. Labels are common-sense names for the columns and rows.

To enter a label, move to the cell in which you want the label to appear, type the label, and press **Enter**.

If an entry is too wide for the column, don't worry. The program will either widen the column automatically or allow you to widen the column later. At this point, part of your entry may not be shown, but when you widen the column, the entire entry will appear.

Not-So-Secret Formulas and Functions

Once you know which items you want the spreadsheet to calculate, you can enter the formulas and functions that will perform the calculations. There's no secret as to how formulas and functions work, as you'll see.

What Are Formulas?

Spreadsheets use formulas to perform calculations on the data you enter. With formulas, you can perform addition, subtraction, multiplication, or division using the values contained in various cells.

Most programs will assume that you want to type a formula if you start your entry with a column letter. Other programs require you to start the formula with a mathematical operator, such as an equal sign (=).

Formulas typically consist of one or more cell addresses and/or values and a mathematical operator, such as + (addition), – (subtraction), * (multiplication), or / (division). For example, if you wanted to determine the average of the three values contained in cells A1, B1, and C1, you would use the following formula:

(A1+B1+C1)/3

To enter a formula, move to the cell in which you want the formula to appear, type the formula, and press **Enter**.

Does It Matter Whether You Add or Divide First?

Most spreadsheet programs perform a series of operations from left to right in the following order, giving some operators *precedence* over others:

1st—exponential equations

2nd—multiplication and division

3rd—addition and subtraction

This is important to keep in mind when you are creating equations, because the order of operations determines the result.

Let's say you want to determine the average of the values in cells A1, B1, and C1, and you enter +A1+B1+C1/3, you'll get the wrong answer. The value in C1 will be divided by 3, and that result will be added to A1+B1. To determine the total of A1 through C1 first, you must enclose that group of values in parentheses: (A1+B1+C1)/3. In most spreadsheet programs, you can use parentheses in this way to change the order of operations.

Lincoln Log Formulas

Because formulas can use the address from any cell containing a value, the formulas can use addresses of cells that contain previous formulas. This is what gives the spreadsheet so much power and flexibility. You don't need one long formula that takes care of everything. The spreadsheet works as you do, breaking the problem into easy pieces that you can put together to build the calculations you need.

Using Ready-Made Formulas for Fancy Calculations

Creating simple formulas (such as adding two numbers) is a piece of cake, but creating a formula for the one-period depreciation of an asset using the straight-line method is a chore. To help you in such cases, many programs offer predefined formulas called *functions*.

Every Function Needs an Argument

Functions are complex ready-made formulas that perform a series of operations on a specified *range* of values. For example, to determine the sum of a series of numbers in cells A1 through H1, you can enter the function @SUM(A1..H1), instead of entering +A1+B1+C1+ and so on. Every function consists of the following three elements:

☛ The @ or = sign indicates that what follows is a function.

☛ The *function name* (for example, SUM) indicates the operation that will be performed.

☛ The *argument*, for example (A1..H1), indicates the cell addresses of the values that the function will act on. The argument is often a range of cells, but it can be much more complex.

Functions for Functions

Some of the more common types of functions are explained in Table 12.1. If you're working with statistical process control, statistical functions are a must. Special accounting programs, such as DacEasy and Peachtree Complete, provide an exhaustive repertoire of financial functions.

Table 12.1   Spreadsheet Functions

Functions	What Kinds of Things They Calculate
Mathematical	Arithmetic calculations, absolute values, logarithms, square roots, and trigonometric equations.
Statistical	Averages, maximum and minimum values, standard deviations and sample variance.
Financial	Compounding periods, internal rate of return, straight-line depreciation allowance, and number of payment periods in an investment.

Form After Function: Making the Cells Look Pretty

Once you have the basic layout of your spreadsheet under control, you can format the cells to give the spreadsheet the desired look.

In most spreadsheet programs, you can enter a command to make the current column as wide as the widest entry in the column. You also can manually adjust the column to make it as wide as your heart (or your number) desires. Likewise, you can adjust the row height, which is usually based on the text size.

Do you want commas inserted in numbers over 999? Do you want to display dollar signs next to monetary values? Do you prefer dates displayed as 09-01-91 or as 09/01/91? Use value formatting to specify how you want numbers displayed.

You can also choose different fonts to emphasize certain cell entries, like column and row headings. A font is a family of characters of the same size and design. For example, Helvetica 12-point is a font. Helvetica is the design (or typestyle), and 12-point is the size. You can also call attention to important information by drawing lines around or between cells, adding shading to cells, or using colors (even white text on a black background for black-and-white printers).

When you've finished designing and formatting your spreadsheet, it's a good idea to save the basic template (labeled rows and columns with formulas entered) in a separate file. That way, whenever you need to enter numbers into the spreadsheet, you'll have a blank form to start with.

Test Driving Your Spreadsheet

When your spreadsheet is complete and you're fairly sure it will work, perform a test run to verify that the spreadsheet meets the following three requirements:

- ☛ You have all the rows and columns you need.
- ☛ The columns are wide enough.
- ☛ The spreadsheet works.

Performing a Test Run

To perform a test run, enter simple numbers in each cell that requires them—numbers that let you calculate the results quickly in your head so you can check the performance of your spreadsheet. Use multiples of ten and be sure to use numbers that are about as wide as the ones you'll be entering.

What Can (and Usually Does) Go Wrong

Even when you're careful, something can go wrong, and it can be difficult to see just what the problem is. If you perform your test run and you're getting an error message or crazy-looking values, check for:

Order of operations   Make sure each formula performs its calculations in the right order. (Remember, you can change the order of calculations by using parentheses.)

Forward references   If you use formulas that rely on other formulas for their calculations, check to make sure that no formula uses the formula in a later cell. In other words, a formula cannot use a value that has not yet been calculated.

Circular references   A circular reference occurs when a formula uses its own results as part of a calculation. The spreadsheet goes around in circles trying to find the answer, but never succeeds.

If something doesn't work, go back and correct it; then perform another test run until the spreadsheet works.

Giving Your Spreadsheet a Bite of Raw Data

When you're certain that your spreadsheet works, get the raw data that you want to calculate and start plugging in the values. When you're done, go back and double-check the values you entered. If the software you are using does not calculate automatically (most do), enter the command to calculate. The spreadsheet quickly displays the results.

Printing and Saving the Finished Spreadsheet

When you finally have all your numbers entered and the spreadsheet has performed the calculations, you may want to print the spreadsheet to send to someone else or to file with your records. And, as usual, you should save your data to disk. The print command and options will vary from program to program.

Put It to Work

At this point, you may be wondering what sorts of things you can use spreadsheets for. The following list will give you some ideas:

Schedules   If you are a project manager, you can use a spreadsheet to keep track of the various projects. You can use a separate row for each project and a separate column for each stage in the project.

Invoices   You can create an invoice that lists the parts delivered, the number of parts, and the price per part. The invoice can calculate the total due for each part, the subtotal of all parts, the amount of sales tax due, and the grand total (total plus tax).

Sales sheets   If you have a product you want to sell, you can use a spreadsheet to show how your product compares with the competition. Use columns to list your product and the various competitive products. Each row can contain information about a feature you want to compare.

Grade sheets   If you are a teacher, you can use a spreadsheet to calculate student averages. You can use a series of formulas to weigh the grades. For example, a final exam grade may count for three test grades.

Inspection results   You can use spreadsheets to create forms for gathering inspection results on an assembly line. For example, you may include a blank for the number of parts per 100 that failed inspection. You can also create a spreadsheet that tallies the results.

Job cost evaluation   For building projects or home improvements, you can create a spreadsheet that compares the various estimates. You use a separate column for each estimate, and you use the rows to compare individual elements of each estimate, such as materials and labor.

Loan amortization   If you are purchasing a house or car or taking out a loan to start your business, you can use a spreadsheet to determine how much interest and principle you will be paying on various loans.

Home or business inventory   Use a spreadsheet to keep track of each item you own and how much it is worth. Such a record is invaluable in the event of a fire or theft. (Assuming the record doesn't get burned or stolen.)

Dropping a Few Spreadsheet Names

There's a spreadsheet program that's right for you, regardless of whether you prefer to use DOS or Windows programs. Lotus 1-2-3 and Quattro Pro are both available in DOS and Windows versions. For Windows connoisseurs, there's Microsoft Excel. And several integrated programs (programs that offer multiple applications) such as Microsoft Works, PFS: First Choice, and PFS: WindowWorks offer spreadsheet modules.

So what are the tradeoffs between DOS and Windows spreadsheets? In general, the Windows spreadsheets offer more powerful features, offer more control over basic features (such as formatting), and are easier to use. Windows spreadsheets also let you link data from one spreadsheet to another. For example, you could link all the data from quarterly sales reports into a year-end report that calculates totals. On the downside, it takes a computer with a lot of memory and hard disk space (and Windows, of course) to run a Windows spreadsheet as fast and efficiently as a DOS spreadsheet.

The Least You Need to Know

This chapter has given you a glimpse of the spreadsheet's power. When you get the opportunity to work with some of the spreadsheets that are on the market, you'll be amazed at how much work they can save you and how fast they perform their chores. Until you get that chance, make sure you understand the basics:

- A spreadsheet is a grid consisting of rows and columns that intersect to form cells.

- Each cell has a unique address that's made up of a letter (representing the column) and a number (representing the row).

- A cell can contain any of the following entries: a row or column heading, a formula, a function with an argument, or a value.

☞ Formulas perform calculations on the values in the cells. Each formula consists of one or more cell addresses and a math operator.

☞ A function is a ready-made complex formula that performs calculations on a range of values.

☞ You can format the cells in a spreadsheet to control the text size and style and to add lines or shading to cells.

☞ Before you begin using your spreadsheet, perform a test run and work out any bugs.

☞ After you enter your data into the spreadsheet, you may have to enter a command to recalculate the spreadsheet.

Chapter 13

Graphics for Business and Pleasure

In This Chapter

- ☛ Creating a business presentation
- ☛ Simple ways to create graphs and flow charts
- ☛ Using ready-made art
- ☛ The difference between paint and draw programs
- ☛ Working with computerized art tools
- ☛ Assembling basic shapes to produce complex illustrations
- ☛ Modifying shapes and objects with the press of a button
- ☛ Using a scanner to copy pictures from paper

In this age of information overload, most of us would rather look at a picture than wade through a sea of words. We don't want to read a newspaper column to find out how many Tomahawk missiles fell on Baghdad. We want a map that shows Baghdad and some little star things that show where the missiles hit, or maybe a graph that shows how many tons of TNT is equal to a missile. Maybe even a dissected view of a missile and how its homing device works. We want *USA Today*.

But what about your presentations and the documents you create? Are you as kind to your audience? Do you use pictures to present information more clearly and succinctly? Do you show as well as tell? After reading this chapter, you will know about several types of programs that will help you answer Yes to all of these questions.

By the Way . . .

In case you're wondering about the structure of this chapter, it basically consists of two parts. In the first part, I show you how to avoid drawing by using prefab graphics. (This is based on the assumption that most people don't have the time to become professional artists.) Later in this chapter, I discuss the graphics programs that require you to have some artistic talent or training.

Getting Down to Business with Graphics

Even if you are not in sales or marketing, you have probably seen a business presentation sometime in your life—probably on TV or in a movie. A sales or marketing representative stands up in front of the board of directors or some other group and shows a series of slides that pitch a new product or show how profitable the company is. How did they create this presentation? Probably by using a presentation graphics program.

Sticking to Business

Presentation graphics programs are based on the assumption that most businesses require only a few graphic elements (often called *charts*): graph charts, text charts, organizational charts, and flow charts. By specializing in business graphics, these programs can expend their programming power on helping you create effective presentations quickly.

Pick a Chart, Any Chart

To create a presentation, you create a series of charts. The first step in creating a chart is to pick a type of chart. Most programs provide a palette of charts from which to choose. You simply type the number of the desired chart or click on it with a mouse.

Some presentation programs refer to each "page" in a presentation as a chart. Other programs call each "page" a *slide* and refer to the presentation as a *slide show*. In this chapter, I use "chart" unless I am referring to a 35mm slide or a chart that is used in an on-screen slide show.

The palette generally offers a text chart (for lists), an organizational chart (for showing the power structure in a company), and several graphs. The type of graph you choose depends on what you want to show. Select a *line graph* to show the progress of data over time (for example, to see if sales are picking up or dropping off). Select a *pie graph* to show the contribution of each part to the whole (for example, to show the contribution of automobile sales to the gross national product). *Bar graphs* are good for comparing data (for example, to see whether Bill or Susan is selling more gizmos this week). And *high-low-close graphs* are useful for seeing how stock prices are doing (you can see the high price for the day, the low price, and the closing price).

Fill in the Blanks

Once you have specified the type of chart you want to create, the program displays a fill-in-the-blank form that requests information. For example, if you choose to create a graph to compare this year's sales figures with last year's figures, you must enter the sales figures you want graphed. The program takes care of the rest and draws the specified chart.

Giving the Chart a Tune-Up

Once you've created a chart, you can dress it up by using the graphics tools included with the program. For example, you can add a title to a graph, add titles to the X and Y axes, add text and change its size, insert a legend to help the user interpret the data, and add arrows and labels to highlight important points.

Some presentation programs (PowerPoint, for instance) include *templates* (ready-made presentations) that were put together by professional artists. These templates specify a background color scheme for each chart, a place for a chart title, and other standard elements. You simply open the template and then change elements to customize it for your own use.

Shuffling Your Slides

Most presentation graphics programs provide a tool that enables you to quickly rearrange the charts in your presentation. Typically, the program displays a screen that shows miniature versions of all the charts. You simply drag the chart where you want it to appear in the presentation or enter numbers for each slide to set their relative positions.

Transforming a Presentation into Something Useful

After you've created a chart or a series of charts, you need to transform your creation into some usable form. For example, you may want to print the charts, convert them into transparencies so you can use them on an overhead projector, or create a slide show that you can display on-screen.

If you want to create slide shows or overhead presentations but you don't have the equipment for making slides and overheads, you can usually send the files to an outside vendor to have the work done. These vendors can transfer your files to 35mm slides, film, or transparencies. Many vendors offer overnight service.

Is a Business Presentation Graphics Program for You?

Many programs offer basic graphics features. For example, several spreadsheet programs (Quattro Pro, Excel, and Lotus) can translate spreadsheet data into graphs. If that's all you need, you would do better purchasing such a program and making use of its advanced spreadsheet features.

If you need the advanced features of a business presentation graphics program, however, there are several good ones out there. For DOS, Harvard Graphics is still top dog. It provides a wide variety of charts, lots of pieces of ready-made art to help you customize each slide, and a complete set of drawing tools.

If you plan on working in Windows, try PowerPoint for Windows. This program is more free wheeling than Harvard Graphics. Instead of selecting a type of chart, each slide starts out with a background and title, and you add various objects to the slides as desired. For example, you might add a bulleted list to one slide, a graph to another, and a drawing to another.

Clip Art: Another Lazy Way to Be Graphic

Unlike business graphics programs (which you've just seen) and paint and draw programs (which you will see later), clip art is not a program. Instead, it is ready-made computer art that was probably created using a graphics program. So, why am I talking about it in a chapter about graphics programs? Because I don't want you to run out and buy a graphics program before you realize that somebody may have already done the drawing for you.

How does clip art work? Say you're creating a newsletter and you want to spruce it up with some pictures. Nothing fancy, maybe a picture of a birthday cake for a column in your company newsletter that announces this month's birthdays. Or, maybe a picture of a baseball player to mark upcoming games for the softball league. Although you might be able to draw the pictures yourself, you can add the art more easily by using *clip art*.

Get It Where You Can: Sources of Clip Art

Some programs come with a collection of clip art on disk. For example, most business presentation programs and paint and draw programs come with clip art. You'll also get a collection of clip art with most desktop publishing programs.

You can also purchase clip art libraries separately on disk, just as you would purchase

Before you buy a clip art library, make sure you have a program that can use the clip art. Some clip art may be in a type of file that your word-processing or desktop publishing program can't use. For example, if you have a word-processing program that can't use PCX files (art created using a program called PC Paintbrush), don't buy a clip art library that consists of PCX images.

a program. These libraries typically include hundreds or thousands of clip art images that are broken down into several categories: borders and backgrounds, computers, communications, people and places, animals, productivity and performance, time and money, travel and entertainment, words and symbols, and more.

Pasting Clip Art on a Page

In many word-processing, desktop publishing, or business presentation programs, you can copy and paste the clip art image from the clip art library onto a page. In other programs, you *import* the image by specifying the name of the file in which the image is saved.

A piece of clip art in WordPerfect for Windows

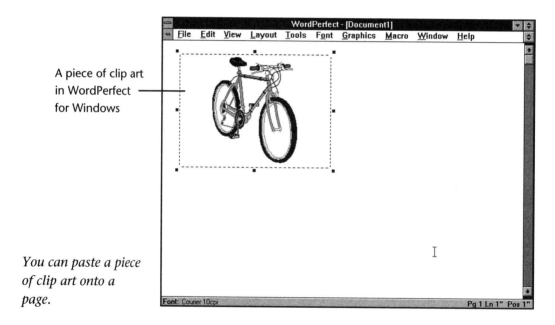

You can paste a piece of clip art onto a page.

Paint and Draw Programs: For Those with Artistic Talent

So, you think you're Leonardo Da Vinci or Georgia O'Keefe. If you have even a smidgen of artistic talent, you can create your own computer art. To create art from scratch, you can use either of two types of graphics programs: a paint program or a draw program.

Computerized Graffiti: Painting on Your Screen

Remember the old Lite Brite toy? It consisted of a box with a lightbulb in it, a peg board, and a bunch of colored, translucent pegs. You stuck the pegs in the board in various patterns to create pictures. The same principle is used for paint programs. You turn on a bunch of on-screen dots to create a picture.

The only difference between a Lite Brite and a paint program is that the paint program comes with a set of tools that give you greater control over the dots (but they don't come with those cool follow-the-dots paper patterns that came with each and every Lite Brite). Most paint programs come with the following tools to help you manipulate the thousands of on-screen pixels:

Your computer screen is essentially a canvas made up of 150,000 to 700,000 tiny lights called *pixels*. Whenever you type a character in a word processing program, or draw a line with a paint or draw program, you activate a series of these pixels so that they form a recognizable shape on-screen.

Spraypaint tool   The spraypaint tool acts like a can of spray paint. You hold down the mouse button and drag the tool across the screen to create a band of paint. Drag the tool fast, and the paint goes on lightly. Drag it slow, and the paint goes on thick.

Paintbrush tool   The paintbrush tool spreads paint evenly across the screen. When you drag the tool across the screen, you get a smooth, uniform ribbon of color.

Mouse Required. If you plan on doing much with graphics, get a mouse. A keyboard is designed for typing text and for moving up, down, left, and right—hardly the fluid movements you need for drawing pictures.

Basic shapes   All paint programs come with a set of shapes: rectangles, circles, lines, and other tools to draw irregular shapes. These tools allow you to stretch a shape to any size or dimension you desire. For example, you can create a small circle or a large oval.

Fill tool   The fill tool allows you to fill a shape with color. You pick the color and then pour it into the shape. The color fills the shape to its outer boundaries.

Color palette   The color palette lets you select the color you want to use for the various tools. For example, if you choose red and then use the spraypaint tool, the paint will come out red.

Thickness palette   The thickness palette lets you select the width of the line created by the selected tool. For example, you can choose to use a wide paintbrush or a narrow one.

Eraser   The eraser works like a chalkboard eraser. You drag it across the screen to remove any unwanted dots. You can zoom in on a portion of your drawing to erase individual dots. (This takes some patience.)

With a paint program, your image is stored as a map of the pixels which make up the image. The map contains a collection of bits; each bit specifies the location and color of one pixel. So, the objects are referred to as *bit-mapped graphics*. Because a bit map contains information for every pixel, bit-mapped files can be very large and require enormous amounts of computer memory.

Zoom tool   If your drawing is too detailed to edit, use the zoom feature to zoom in for a close-up view. If you zoom in close enough, the program enables you to edit individual pixels. When you've finished editing that portion of the illustration, zoom out again to see the big picture.

Using the Drawing and Painting Tools

If you want to draw a shape or drag a ribbon of paint across the screen, you first select the tool, a color, and a line thickness. You then roll the mouse (or other drawing device) on your desk until the mouse pointer is where you want the shape or line to begin, and press the mouse button. (This beginning point is called the *anchor point*.) As you hold down the mouse button and drag the mouse pointer away from the anchor point, the object gets stretched out between the anchor point and the mouse pointer.

Playing with Shapes Using a Draw Program

A draw program lets you create drawings by putting together a bunch of shapes. For example, you might draw a city-scape by putting together a bunch of rectangles of various sizes and dimensions.

Draw programs are often called *object-oriented* graphics programs, because they treat objects as individual units rather than as a collection of pixels.

Getting a Handle on Graphics Objects

Once you've drawn an object, handles appear around the object. You can then drag the object anywhere on-screen or change the object's shape, size, or orientation without affecting surrounding objects.

To move an object, click on the object with your mouse. (Handles appear around the object.) Move the mouse pointer over the center of the object (not on any of the handles). Hold down the mouse button and drag the object to the desired location.

To change an object's size or dimensions, click on the object with your mouse. Move the mouse pointer over one of the handles and hold down the mouse button (this is commonly called *grabbing* a handle). Drag the handle toward the center of the object to make it smaller or narrower, or away from the center to make it larger or wider.

Shapes, Together and Apart

In a paint program, if you lay a circle on top of a square, the circle and square become one. Wherever their lines cross, they are linked like Siamese twins. With a draw program, objects retain their autonomy. If you lay a

Unlike paint programs, which keep track of objects pixel-by-pixel, draw programs store each graphic object as a mathematical formula. The formula contains codes which tell the program how to display and print the object. For example, the formula for a circle might contain the position of the circle's center and the diameter of the circle.

circle on a square, you can later pull the circle off the square just as if it had been drawn on a separate tansparency.

However, you do have the option of treating the objects as a unit. To group several objects, you typically draw a selection box around the objects. You can then move, copy, or delete the group of objects as if they were a single object.

Which Is Better: Paint or Draw?

Because paint programs give you control over individual pixels, they are especially useful for drawing irregular lines and using fine grades of shading. This makes paint programs useful for drawing freehand sketches and creating realistic-looking images. Popular IBM paint programs include PC Paintbrush and Publisher's Paintbrush.

Draw programs are useful for creating simple or complex drawings consisting of basic geometric shapes and straight lines. This makes drawing programs especially useful for technical illustrations, advertisements, and logos. Popular draw programs include CorelDRAW! and Windows Draw!.

What About Text?

Although paint and draw programs are not designed to handle huge blocks of text, they do let you add labels and draw arrows to point out important areas of an illustration.

Paint programs handle text as a series of pixels, making the text very difficult to edit. The process may require you to cut a portion of the text and paste in a revised portion. Aligning the revised text can be extremely frustrating. Draw programs offer much more flexibility when dealing with text. The text is contained in a separate box, and you can edit the text just as if you were using a word-processing program.

Adding Photos and Figures to Your Masterpiece

If you have a photograph or a drawing on paper, and if you have the right equipment, you can turn your existing photos into pixel versions. To do this, you need a digitizer or a scanner that converts the image into a series of dots and stores it on a disk. You also must have a graphics program that supports a scanner (the scanner usually comes with a program). Once the image is in your system, you can edit it in your favorite paint program.

The Least You Need to Know

Graphics can get as complex as you like. With an advanced graphics program, you can create three-dimensional, life-like drawings that look like sleek color photos in a magazine ad. But for now, just make sure you know the basics:

- ☛ A business presentation consists of a collection of charts.

- ☛ To create a chart in a business presentation graphics program, you select the chart and then enter the data you want to chart.

- ☛ Clip art images are small pieces of ready-made art that you can include in your presentations and publications.

- ☛ A paint program allows you to create freehand sketches and other intricate drawings.

- ☛ In a paint program, you have full control over each pixel on the screen.

- ☛ A draw program treats each object on-screen as an individual element.

- ☛ In a draw program, you assemble shapes to create an illustration.

- ☛ Draw programs are typically used to create floor plans, technical illustrations, and other drawings that consist of regular, geometric shapes.

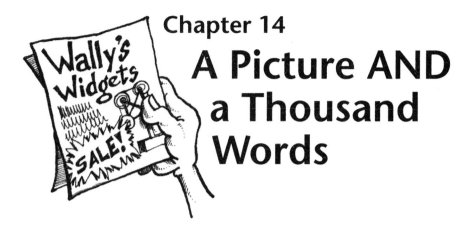

Chapter 14

A Picture AND a Thousand Words

In This Chapter

- ☞ How to combine graphics and text on the same page
- ☞ Changing the size and style of type
- ☞ Dragging text around on a page
- ☞ Squeezing and stretching columns of text
- ☞ Wrapping text around graphics
- ☞ Squeezing and stretching graphic objects on-screen
- ☞ Accenting your document with lines and other basic shapes

Every day you get a handful of them in the mail: slick, colorful brochures and flyers asking you to buy Wally's Widgets or join the Stocking Cap of the Month club. These wonderful creations bring visions to your mind of artists laboring for hours with pots of glue, pasting every letter and graphic into exactly the right place before dashing off with the piece to a printer. Well, my friend, desktop publishing programs have put those days to rest.

With a desktop publishing (DTP) program, you take bits of text and graphics and slap them on the page. Drag the text and graphics on-screen, plop them down where you want them, and rearrange at will. No messy glue, no scissors, and no running out to the printer.

Blank Stares at a Blank Page

When you start a desktop publishing program, don't expect the program to jump up and offer help (although some do). You get a blank page, just like you get in any program. Your job is to start pasting little scraps of text and pictures on the page, just as if you were creating a collage.

The blank space around the page acts as a *paste-up board*. You can use this area to temporarily store scraps of text and pictures. For example, if you want to move a picture from one page to the next, you can drag the picture off the page and set it on the paste-up board. Turn to the page on which you want the picture to appear, and then drag the picture from the paste-up board onto the page.

In addition to a paste-up board, a desktop publishing screen typically contains a horizontal and vertical ruler to help you align the text and graphics, a pull-down menu for entering commands, and a toolbox, containing some tools for working with graphics and text.

Bringing in the Text

Although you can create text directly in a desktop publishing program, you may save time by typing the text first in your word-processing program. This allows you to use the advanced features of your word-processing program (such as the spell checker and search and replace) to edit the text. You can then *import* the text into your desktop publishing program.

> ### By the Way . . .
> Most desktop publishing programs can use files created by the more popular word-processing programs—WordPerfect, Microsoft Word, and WordStar. If you are using a less popular program, you can save the document as an ASCII file (a plain-text file) in your word-processing program.

Making a Box to Hold Your Text

In most desktop publishing programs, you must create a *text box* before you can place text on a page. The text box acts as a receptacle for the text, allowing you to "pour" text into the box, and preventing the text from spilling over onto other parts of the page. (Some less advanced programs do not use text boxes.)

To create a text box, you click on the text box tool and then use the mouse to drag a text box to the desired size and dimensions. (Don't worry about whether or not the text will fit inside the box, you can resize the box later.) The text box is usually defined by a dotted line.

Pouring in the Text

A text box is like a coffee cup; it is empty until you "pour" something into it. Once you've created a text box, enter the command for importing the text. The program prompts you to specify the location, name, and format of the text file. Once you enter the appropriate information, the program retrieves the text into the text box.

If the text does not fit in the text box, some of the text may not be shown, or the program will give you the option of *spilling* the text that won't fit into another text box. In either case, don't worry if you can't see part of the text; it's still there.

Squeezing and Stretching the Text Box

A text box is like an accordion without the folds. You can squeeze it to make a column of text more narrow, or stretch it to make the column wider. To do this, you click on the text box. Small rectangles, called *handles*, appear around the box. With the mouse, drag a handle to move the side or corner of the box to change its size or dimensions.

In programs that don't use text boxes, you can control the column width of the text by changing the margins, just as you would in a word-processing program.

A *font* is any set of characters of the same *typeface* (design) and *type size* (measured in points). For example, Times Roman 12-point is a font; Times Roman is the typeface, and 12-point is the size. (There are 72 points in an inch.) Following are some examples of fonts:

Century Schoolbook 18-point

`OCR/B 10-point`

Helvetica 12-point

Times 9-point

Text Box on Wheels

The neat thing about electronic paste-up is that you don't have to rip something off the page to move it; you simply drag the item where you want it. Click on the text box to select it, and then move the mouse pointer over an edge of the text box (but not over a handle). In most programs, the mouse pointer turns into a four-headed arrow, which means you can move the box in any of four directions. Hold down the mouse button and drag the box where you want it.

Making Your Text Look Its Best

When you bring text into a document, it looks fairly drab—nothing like the fancy print you see in magazines. In order to bring the text to life, you must *format* the text. In the next few sections, you will learn what's involved in formatting.

Fontastic Looking Type

Most desktop publishing programs offer a variety of *fonts* you can use to emphasize a word or phrase, to set headings apart from surrounding text, or simply to give text a certain look.

In most programs, changing a font is a two-step process. First you select the text whose font you want to change by dragging the mouse pointer over it. Then, you select the desired font, usually from a pull-down menu.

Lookin' Good: Enhancing Your Text

In addition to changing fonts, you can *enhance* text by making the text bold, italic, underlined, or some other variation of the font. When you enhance text, the text's font stays the same, but an aspect of the type is changed. Most programs offer the following enhancements:

Plain	This is the default, the same as having no enhancement.
Bold	**Bold adds emphasis. Use bold to introduce important points, such as Note: or Tip:, or for section headings. Use bold sparingly or it loses its impact.**
Italic	*Italic is used to set off key phrases or words. Because italic isn't as strong as bold print, it's usually safer to use.*
Outline	Outline provides an outline around the character. It's a fancier enhancement, used for cards, newsletter headlines, and announcements.
Shadow	Shadow shades around the base of characters to give them a three-dimensional look. This is another fancy enhancement that makes the characters look more like graphic elements.
Condense	Condense prints tiny characters. This is an excellent choice for footnotes or other text that you want to include without detracting from the main text.
Overstrike	**Overstrike is a lot like bold, except that it gives your letter a double-image look.**

When using different fonts, make sure your printer can print them; otherwise, the font may appear on-screen, but it might not be printed.

You use fonts and enhancements together to emphasize or set off a word or phrase. For example, you could use Times Roman 12-point italic when introducing a new term. Or you might use Helvetica 16-point shadow to create a fancy headline.

Getting Uptight or Shaking Loose

To keep two lines of text from crashing into one another, extra space, called *leading* (pronounced LEDing), is inserted between the lines. The more leading you have, the farther apart the lines of text are. Leading is measured in points and is usually added to the type size to determine overall spacing from the bottom of one line to the bottom of the next line (baseline to baseline). For example, in most programs, if you're using a type size of 10, the program automatically adds two points of leading between each line. The baseline-to-baseline measurement in this case is 12 points (10-point type + 2-point leading).

By the Way . . .

Leading is a beautiful thing. You can use it to subtly make a report look longer. For example, if you need a 5-page report, and you can only come up with 4 pages of text, increase the leading to get the extra page. You can also use leading to make your resume more balanced. If you have just over 1 page, decrease the leading to fit it on one page. If you have a page and a half, increase the leading to fill the second page. Adding extra leading after each paragraph also gives your documents a more professional look.

Tighten That Text!

Kerning means reducing the space between individual characters. Without kerning, certain letters within words may look unevenly spaced—some characters may be far apart while others nearly overlap. Kerning lets you adjust the spacing between letters so your words look attractive, especially for large type sizes such as those used in headlines.

What About the Box?

In addition to styling the text inside the text box, you can style the text box itself. Most programs let you shade inside the box, add a line around the box, or add a drop-shadow that makes the box look as though it is lifted above the page.

Fast Formatting with Styles

Desktop publishing programs, like word-processing programs, often use styles to simplify the task of formatting the text of your document. A style is a name assigned to a collection of formatting settings.

To understand styles, consider the following example. You are creating a book, and each chapter title is to be set in the font 24-point New Century Schoolbook, set in italic, and indented five spaces from the right margin. Rather than change the font, style, indentation, and point size each time you type a chapter title, you can create a style called Chapter Title. This style would contain all the specified format settings. The next time you need to format a chapter title, you highlight the chapter title and choose the Chapter Title style.

Another advantage of using styles is that you can quickly change the formatting of all the text formatted with a particular style. Suppose you decide that the chapter title should be larger, say 36-point type. Because you formatted all the chapter titles with the Chapter Title style, you can edit the style, changing the point size from 24 to 36. When you are finished editing, all the chapter titles that were formatted with the Chapter Title style are changed to 36-point type.

What About Graphics?

Although you will spend most of your time working with text, the real power of a desktop publishing program is that it lets you place graphic elements on the page, as well. What kind of graphic elements? The following list explains some common graphic elements you can put on a page:

Most desktop publishing programs can use files if they have been saved in a standard graphics format. For IBM programs, the most common file formats are PCX, TIFF, and BMP. If your desktop publishing program does not support a particular format, you will not be able to import a file that has been saved in that format.

Pictures created in a paint or draw program   If you have a paint or draw program, you can create an illustration and import it into your document.

Clip art drawings   Many desktop publishing programs come with a collection of clip art that you can use to accent your publications. You can also purchase clip art separately.

Scanned images   If you have a scanner, you can scan an image or photo from paper, save it as a file, and import the scanned image into your document.

Lines, circles, and rectangles   Most desktop publishing programs have tools for drawing basic shapes, such as lines, circles, and rectangles. These objects let you provide visual devices for dividing the text on a page.

Picture This: Graphics in Your Document

Although you can create basic graphic elements, such as lines and boxes, from within the desktop publishing program, you cannot create the complex illustrations that you can generate with a draw or paint program. Because of that, you will likely import existing pictures into the desktop publishing document.

Some desktop publishing programs allow you to create a graphics box and then import a picture into the box. This can distort the image. For example, if you have a picture of a tall, thin man and you import him into a short, wide box, you end up with a picture of a short, fat man. In other words, the box makes the man.

To place a graphic image, you normally enter the command for importing a graphic image. The program prompts you to specify the location and name of the graphics file and the format in which the file was saved. Once you enter the appropriate information, the program retrieves the image and displays it on-screen in a graphics box. A graphics box is just like a text box except that it contains a picture rather than text.

Squeezing and Stretching the Picture

Once you have your picture on-screen, you can resize it or move it. When you select the image, handles appear around it, just as with a text box. You can drag the handles or drag a side of the box to reshape or move the box. Most programs allow you to change the shape of the box without messing up the relative dimensions of the picture.

Drawing Lines and Shapes

In addition to full-fledged pictures, you can add lines, circles, and rectangles to a publication to break up the text, to separate columns of text, or simply to make the page look more graphic.

To add a line or a basic shape, you first select the line or shape you want to draw. (You can usually select the line width you want.) Move the mouse pointer where you want the line or shape to begin, hold down the mouse button, and drag the mouse until the line is the desired length or until the shape is of the desired size and dimensions. When you release the mouse button, the shape appears on-screen.

Around You Go

This chapter makes desktop publishing sound like a linear process: you drop in some text, design the text, add a few pictures and lines, and you're ready to print. In fact, the process is much more circular. You'll place some text, design it, and then place a graphic image next to it. When you look at the page, the type may appear too small next to the image, or the image may not be quite where you want it.

With a desktop publishing program, making adjustments is easy. You can fiddle with the page as much as you like, sizing and resizing the graphic images, adding or deleting lines, making columns wider or more narrow. You have complete control over the page.

Stacking and Unstacking Objects

When you lay objects on a page, you eventually get overlapping objects, like a stack of pancakes. With pancakes, you can't eat the one on the bottom unless you move it to the top or move the other pancakes off it. The same is true with text and graphics objects on a page. If you try to click on an object that's on the bottom of the stack, you end up selecting the object on top.

To help in such cases, most DTP programs contain commands that let you move an object to the front, move it to the back, or move it up one level in the stack.

A desktop publishing program called Microsoft Publisher (for Windows) has a feature called PageWizards that leads you through the creation of a variety of publications. You choose the type of publication you want (greeting card, newsletter, business card), and the PageWizard asks you a series of questions (like how big you want the headline. whether you want a picture on the front, and so on). When you finish answering the questions, the PageWizard creates the publication to your exact specifications! For lazy folks like me, Page-Wizards are a godsend.

Page Layout for the Stylistically Impaired

Desktop publishing programs offer several features to help you lay out pages more consistently and accurately. These features include *master pages* and *grids*.

A *master page* contains a collection of elements that will appear on every page in the publication. For example, a master page may contain a company logo, a page number, a chapter title, and a horizontal line across the top of the page.

When you print the publication, the elements are printed on every page of the publication in the same location on every page. If you do not want to use the text or graphics from a master page, you can turn it off for certain pages.

A *grid* is like a transparent piece of graph paper that allows you to align text and graphics precisely on a page. Many programs include a *snap to* grid. When you move text or graphics on the grid, the snap to feature snaps the object to the nearest grid line for consistent alignment.

Desktop Publishing Programs— Are They All the Same?

What separates one desktop publishing program from another are the number and type of features each offers. Some programs are great for designing single pages for brochures and newsletters, but they just don't offer the comprehensive features required for publishing long documents that contain repetitive page layouts, like books.

When looking at different programs, decide what types of publications you need to produce. If you want to create greeting cards, resumes, newsletters, business cards, and other short publications, programs like PFS: First Publisher, Microsoft Publisher, and Express Publisher offer enough basic features to get the job done without overwhelming you with complexity.

For more intensive work, a program like PageMaker, Ventura Publisher, or Quark XPress provides more features for refining the appearance of your pages.

By the Way . . .

When you are shopping for a desktop publishing program, you're better off with a program that runs under Microsoft Windows. These programs generally give you more control over text and graphics.

Do You Even Need a Desktop Publishing Program?

If you don't want to invest the time and money learning to use a desktop publishing program, try a full-featured word-processing program, such as WordPerfect, Microsoft Word for Windows, or Ami Pro. These advanced word-processing programs support several fonts and typestyles, allow you to import graphics, let you preview pages, and provide line drawing tools for accenting your documents.

Although you won't have the same amount of control over text and graphics as you'll find in a desktop publishing program, you will still be able to get the job done.

The Least You Need to Know

In this chapter, you learn a great deal about desktop publishing, including some advanced information about typesetting. Although all this information is vitally important, some facts are more important than others:

☞ Desktop publishing programs combine text and graphics from other programs to form fully illustrated pages.

☞ Although desktop publishing programs do let you type text and create graphic images, their main purpose is to *manage* the text and graphics that are created in the full-featured word-processing and graphics programs.

☞ When you import text into most desktop publishing programs, the text is placed in a text box.

☞ When you import a graphic image into a desktop publishing program, the image appears in a graphics box.

☞ You can move an object on the screen by dragging it with the mouse.

☞ When you select an object, handles appear around it. You can drag a handle to change the size and dimensions of the object.

☞ You can save a group of format settings as a style and use the style to apply the formats quickly and consistently.

☞ Master pages let you create text and graphics to appear on every page of a document.

☞ Some desktop publishing programs can display a grid that helps you align the objects on a page.

☞ Many word processors provide basic desktop publishing features, supporting several fonts and letting you create basic graphic images.

Chapter 15

"One Ringy-Dingy, Two Ringy-Dingies..." Dialing Out with Your PC

In This Chapter

☛ Subscribing to an on-line service

☛ Communicating with others through electronic mail

☛ Shopping with your computer

☛ The hardware and software you need to get started

☛ Understanding the difference between internal and external modems

☛ How to install another phone jack for your modem

☛ How to install an external modem

☛ What you can do with a modem, and the type of software you need to do it

☛ Telecommunications settings: What they are and why you need to know them

How would you like to play a computer game against a friend in another town? Look up books at the local library while sitting at your desk? Check the news and weather or look up an encyclopedia article by pecking away on your keyboard? Order items from a computerized catalogue? Or even transfer files from your computer to a colleague's computer anywhere in

TECHNO NERD TEACHES

Modem stands for MOdulator/DEModulator. To send information, the modem *modulates* (translates) the computer data into a form which can be sent through the phone lines. To receive information, the modem *demodulates* the incoming information, translating it into a form which your computer can understand.

the world? In this chapter, you'll learn how you can do all this with your computer, a modem, and the proper software.

Connecting to the Outside World

One of the first things most people do with a modem is connect to an on-line service, such as Prodigy, CompuServe, America Online, or the Dow Jones News Retrieval. You subscribe to the service (usually for 10 to 15 dollars a month). You get a program that allows you to connect locally to the service, and you get access to what the service offers. In the next few sections, you'll see what these services offer.

Paperless Newspapers, Magazines, and More

Most on-line services provide files you can download and allow you to buy and sell stocks, shop, make travel reservations, and access encyclopedias, newspapers, or magazine articles from around the world.

SPEAK LIKE A GEEK

"Download" is a fancy term that means "copy." When you download a file, you copy it from the service to your computer.

What's the downside? First, you don't get many pictures. If you look up something in the encyclopedia, you get only text. The newspaper offers the same. Also, with most newspapers, you get only a smattering of news—usually the front page of the national news and the front page of the local news. If you like to take a leisurely flip through the newspaper while drinking your first morning cup of coffee, don't cancel your subscription just yet.

Meeting People with Similar Interests

A lot of people subscribe to on-line information services, such as Prodigy and America Online. On-line services frequently offer forums where people with special interests can chat on line or post messages. This puts you in touch with a wide range of people, many of whom share your interests. Whether you are interested in restoring old cars, growing beautiful flower gardens, or hacking away on your computer, you can find someone out there who is doing the same thing. You can discuss your interests, seek help for a problem you are currently trying to solve, offer help to a colleague, or just share funny stories.

Postage-Free Mail, Same-Day Delivery

How would you like to write and send a letter and have it reach its destination in less than a minute? With electronic mail (E-mail for short), you can have this warp-speed delivery. When you subscribe to an on-line service (or a separate E-mail service), you can send E-mail to other subscribers of the service. You also get your own electronic mailbox that can store messages sent by other users.

The Ultimate in Home Shopping

Prodigy and other on-line services are packed with companies that are thirsty for your business and who make ordering a list of items as simple as pressing a few keys (it's almost too easy). You can order furniture, clothes, software, computer gadgets, compact discs, movies, and anything else you have a yen (or a dollar) for. As long as you have a credit card that's not maxed out, you can order anything you need—and many things you don't need.

Kid Stuff

If you have kids, they can get a lot out of an on-line service as well. Kids can read the classic children's stories and magazine articles written just for kids. If the child needs to write a report for school, he or she can access the on-line encyclopedia, read the latest news in science, or get a rundown of current events. Most on-line services also offer games.

Keep tabs on your phone bill. If you use a modem to call long-distance, your friendly neighborhood phone company charges you long-distance rates, so keep this in mind when you are chatting on the modem. Most on-line information services, however, provide you with a local number for connecting to the service. You can then communicate with other people in different states by way of the local connection.

The Price You Pay for All of This

When you're shopping for an on-line service, compare subscription rates. For example, Prodigy charges a flat monthly rate (about $15) that allows you to use the service as much as you want during the month and send up to 30 E-mail messages per month. Additional messages cost 25 cents each. With America Online, you pay a flat rate (about $10) for three hours a month, $5 for each additional hour at night or on weekends, and $10 for each additional hour during the weekdays.

Local Bulletin Boards (That You Don't Find in Schools or Supermarkets)

If you don't want to pay a subscription price to an on-line service, you may be able to connect to a local bulletin board for free or for a fraction of the cost. Don't expect to get the fancy features of costly on-line service, but the local bulletin board may let you share files with local computer users, make valuable local contacts, and get help for your computer woes. To find out about local bulletin boards, call around to various computer dealers. If they don't know of any local bulletin boards, they may know of some computer clubs you can ask. You may even want to set up your own bulletin board.

Person-to-Person Calls

You don't have to subscribe to an on-line service in order to communicate with another computer user. If you and a friend or colleague each have a modem and a telecommunications program (you don't have to have the same program), you can communicate and transfer files through the phone lines. (You'll learn more about the type of program you need to do this later.)

Remote Computing

How would you like to take control of your office computer from your home computer? With a remote computing program, you can connect the two computers, via modem, and use a program installed on your office computer to edit one of the documents stored on its hard disk. If you forgot to bring a file home, simply call your office computer and download the file from its hard disk.

To take advantage of remote computing, you must have the same remote computing program running on both computers. These programs include Carbon Copy, PC Anywhere, and Commute (included with the utility program PC Tools). The computer you want to call must be set up to wait for your call. You can then call the remote computer, establish the connection, and start using it.

Remote computing programs come with a feature that allows you to screen calls. Some programs, for example, have a *call-back* feature. When you call the computer and give it your password, the computer hangs up and then calls you back at the phone number associated with your password. This prevents undesirables from calling your computer and messing it up.

What You'll Need to Get Started

Before you can start placing calls, you'll need to get a modem, some communications software, and an open phone jack (place where you plug in the phone).

When shopping for a modem, you'll need to choose between an *internal* or an *external* modem. An internal modem is a board that plugs into an expansion slot inside your computer. To use an internal modem, you must have an open expansion slot inside your computer. An external modem plugs into a serial port (a receptacle) on the back of your computer. To use an external modem, you must have an extra serial port; if the mouse is plugged into your only serial port, you'll have to unplug it.

SPEAK LIKE A GEEK

Serial ports are also referred to as COM (Communications) ports. These ports are numbered COM1, COM2, COM3, and COM4. You'll learn why this is important later.

Inside your computer is the mother of all circuit boards, appropriately called the *motherboard*. This board contains some openings called *expansion slots* that allow you to add items to the motherboard. If you buy an internal modem, you must plug it into an expansion slot. You can then connect the phone line to the modem. (Chapter 18 tells you more about such mumbo jumbo as expansion slots.)

OOPS!

Many fax/modems are able only to send faxes, not to receive them. If you want to be able to receive faxes, make sure the fax/modem can handle incoming faxes. Also, make sure your modem supports Group III fax machines. Nearly 90 percent of faxes in use today are of the Group III variety.

In addition to a modem, your computer needs instructions that tell it how to communicate using the modem; this is what communications software does. Most modems come with such a program, but you usually need a more sophisticated program, such as PROCOMM PLUS or the telecommunications program that comes with Windows.

The final thing you need is a phone jack. You will plug the modem into a phone jack, just like a telephone. If you don't have a phone jack near your computer, you'll have to install an additional jack or move your computer. You'll learn how to install a phone jack later.

Internal or External?

Get an internal modem if you have room inside your computer and you plan to use the modem on only one computer; otherwise, get an external modem. Also, make sure the modem is *Hayes compatible* and communicates at at least 2400 baud—9600 baud is even better. (You'll learn about baud later.)

To Fax or Not to Fax

Some modems, called fax modems, come equipped with the ability to send faxes or send and receive faxes. Just as with fully equipped fax machines, a fax/modem allows you to dial a number and transmit pages of text, graphics, and charts to a conventional fax machine, or to another computer that has a fax/modem.

The trouble with fax modems is that they don't let you feed a piece of paper through the machine. So say your doctor tells you to fax a copy of your insurance card to her, you're out of luck. If you had a scanner, you could scan the card into your computer and then send it, but that's hardly a time-saver.

Another problem with fax modems is that you have to keep your computer on all the time in order to receive a fax, unless of course you know exactly when the person is going to send the fax. This could get more expensive than going out and buying a separate fax machine.

Wait a Minute, Jack: Do You Need Another Plug for the Modem?

Before you install a phone jack, you have to ask yourself whether or not you *need* to install one. This depends on whether or not you have a phone jack near the computer.

TECHNO NERD TEACHES

The Hayes modem, made by a company called Hayes Technologies, has set the standard in the modem market. Hayes modems use a set of commands that allow you to tell the modem what you want it to do and how you want it to operate. (For example, to dial the phone number 567-1234, you would enter the Hayes command ATDT followed by the phone number.) This set of commands is called the *Hayes command set.* When a modem is advertised as being Hayes-compatible, it means that the modem can understand Hayes commands. Many communications programs automatically enter Hayes commands for you.

If you already have a phone jack near the computer, but your phone is plugged into it, you don't need to install an additional jack. Your first option is to get a modem with two phone jacks. Most modems come with two phone jacks—one that connects the modem to the incoming phone line and another into which you can plug your phone. When you are not using the modem, you can use the phone as you normally would.

If you don't have a modem with two phone jacks, you can purchase a split phone connector from an electronics store that allows you to plug your phone and modem into the same jack.

If Your Computer Is Far from a Phone Jack

If your computer is far from any phone jack, you can install an additional jack by running a wire from one of your current jacks to your computer. You don't have to be an electrician to install a phone jack. You can get the necessary supplies (the phone wire and a new jack) from any electronics store, and if you know how to use a screwdriver (and maybe a drill), you should be able to install the jack in less than an hour.

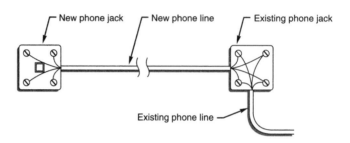

To install another phone jack, you branch off from an existing jack.

By the Way . . .

Your modem is just like another member of the family. If your modem is on the line, you won't be able to use the phone, and nobody will be able to call you. If you want to be able to use the phone while the modem is using it, you will have to call the telephone company and have them install a separate (data) line, with its own phone number.

Installing a Modem

Modem installation varies depending on whether you are installing an internal or external modem. With an internal modem, you must get under the hood of your PC, plug the modem into an open expansion slot, and plug the modem into the phone jack. If you're a rank beginner, don't try this alone. Ask a computer geek friend to help you, or take your computer to a dealer to have the modem installed.

Just about anyone can install an external modem. All you have to do is make three connections. First, connect the modem to the serial port on your computer using a serial cable. Next, plug the modem's power cord into a receptacle on your wall or into a power strip or surge suppressor. Finally, connect the modem to the phone jack. This is just like plugging a phone into a phone jack. (You might also want to connect your phone to the modem, as shown here.)

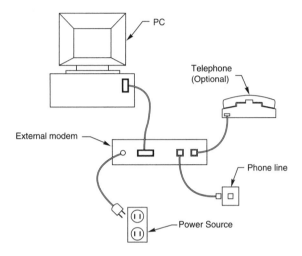

An external modem requires three connections.

Hold On a Minute . . . You May Need Another Program

Before you can place a call using your modem, you need to know a little bit about the programs that make telecommunications possible, because you may need another program to accomplish what you're setting out to do. Ask yourself what you want to do with the modem. Then read on to learn more about some of the common uses for a modem and the type of program (in addition to your communications program) required for each use.

Do you want to hook into an on-line information service (such as Prodigy or America Online)? If you do, you have to purchase a special program and then pay the

If you have your modem and phone on the same line, your modem will try to answer the phone when it rings. (This drives my wife crazy.) To get around the problem, you can buy a voice/data switch that routes the call to your computer or phone. If the incoming call is one of those high-pitched computer squeals, the switch routes the call to the computer. If the call is a normal phone call, your phone rings so you can pick it up and start talking.

SPEAK LIKE A GEEK

What's a *bulletin board system*? A bulletin board system (BBS for short) enables a computer to automatically answer the phone when other computers call. The BBS allows the calling computer to copy files to it (*upload* files) and copy files from it (*download* files). Although you can purchase a BBS program to set up your own BBS, most users work with BBS's set up by computer companies and professional associations.

subscription price to the service. (You can usually get the program free or very cheap, because most of these places want you to try their service.)

Do you want to play a computer game in two-player mode? Some game programs, such as *Populous*, allow you to play in two-player mode. That is, you can connect to another computer with a modem, and play against the person running the other computer. If the program documentation says you can play in two-player mode, then it already contains the software tools you'll need to play the game over the phone lines. All you need to add is a modem—and an opponent who owns a copy of the same game.

If you want to transfer files between two computers or connect to a bulletin board system, you need a communications program. Most modems come with a simple communications program. If you have PC Tools, Windows, or some other integrated program (see Chapter 17), it may come with a communications program. You can also purchase advanced communications programs, such as PROCOMM PLUS.

If you have two computers you want to connect for remote computing, you'll need a remote computing program for each computer. Say you have a computer at work and one at home. You can purchase a special remote computing program that will let you control your computer at work from your computer at home and vice versa.

Telecommunications Settings . . . What Telecommunications Settings?

If you connect your computer to another computer or to an on-line service, you must make sure both computers are using the same *communications settings*. Otherwise, errors may result during data transfer. For example, if one modem is talking at 9600 baud and the other is listening

at 2400 baud, it is likely that some information will get lost. Common communications
settings include the following:

Baud rate   The speed at which the two
modems transfer data. The transfer can
only be as fast as the slower of the two
modems allows. Baud rate is commonly
measured in bits per second (bps).

Parity   Tests the integrity of the data sent
and received. Common setting is None or
No Parity.

Data bits   Indicates the number of bits in
each transmitted character. Common
setting is Eight.

Stop bits   Indicates the number of bits
used to signal the end of a character.
Common setting is One bit.

Duplex   Tells the computer whether to
send and receive data at the same time (Full), or send data or receive
data but not both at the same time (Half). Common setting is Full.

The important thing to remember is that the communications settings
must be the same on both computers. Once the settings are right, you can
enter a command to have the modem call the other computer. The communications program will dial the number and establish the connection
between the two computers.

TECHNO NERD TEACHES

What's the difference
between baud and bits per
second? *Baud* is the maximum number of times a
modem can change the
signal it sends per second.
Bits per second refers to the
number of bits of information transferred per second.
A modem may send more
than one bit of information
for each change in the
electrical signal. For example, a modem operating
at 300 baud may be trans-
ferring at 1200 bps. So if
you are comparison shop-
ping, you would do better
to compare rates based on
bits per second.

Safe Computing: How to Avoid Evil Computer Viruses

Whenever you connect your computer to another computer, you take a
risk of contracting a computer virus. However, as long as you connect to
legitimate services and you only download files from safe bulletin board
systems, the risks are small. If you download program files from a bulletin

board or information service and run the programs on your computer, your system is slightly more at risk. If you download only data files (news articles, letters from friends), you run almost no risk of contracting a computer virus.

If you are worried about viruses, get yourself a good virus protection program, as explained in Chapter 21, and scan your system for viruses on a regular basis.

The Least You Need to Know

By connecting your computer to other computers, you can tap the power and resources of another computer in another part of your company, across town, or anywhere in the world. When you begin using your computer to communicate with the world, keep in mind that:

- ☞ Bulletin board systems (BBSs) let other people call your computer to leave and read messages and transfer files.

- ☞ In order for two modems to communicate, they must be using the same communication settings.

- ☞ Telecommunications deals with connecting computers via modem through telephone lines.

- ☞ To communicate through the phone lines, you need a modem, a telecommunications program, and an open phone jack.

- ☞ The speed at which a modem transfers information is measured in bits per second.

- ☞ The telecommunications program you need depends on what you want to do. When you subscribe to an on-line service, you usually get the program you need in order to connect to the service.

Chapter 16

Counting Your Chickens: Time and Money Management

In This Chapter

- Using your computer to write and print checks
- Making a computer balance your checkbook
- Managing a budget on your computer
- Programs that can help you plan your financial future
- Accounting programs for large and small businesses
- Using a calendar program to keep track of important dates
- Keeping track of things to do

Computers are naturals when it comes to accounting and date-keeping. This chapter introduces three types of software that can help you manage your time and money.

Personal finance programs can help you balance your checkbook, keep track of credit card charges, and manage a budget. *Accounting programs* can help you manage money in a business setting. And *Calendar programs* keep track of important dates, appointments, and upcoming projects.

SPEAK LIKE A GEEK

Personal finance programs are often called *check-writing* programs, because their main purpose is to help you keep a balanced checkbook. However, these programs are becoming more diverse. Some personal finance programs can be used to manage the finances of a small business, and others (such as WealthStarter) contain tools for teaching you how to invest your money intelligently.

Getting Personal with Your Finances

The only thing personal about finances is that you have to take a personal interest in your finances in order to keep from going broke. Few people actually enjoy balancing checkbooks and figuring budgets. However, personal finance programs can help make these jobs a little less painful.

The Perils of Writing Checks by Hand

The problem with writing checks is that you have to enter a lot of duplicate information. You write the date on the check, the name of the person or business the check is for, the amount of the check (both numerically and spelled out), and a memo telling what the check is for. Then, you flip to your check register and enter all the same information again. If you happen to make a mistake copying the amount from your check to your register, you'll have lots of fun balancing your checkbook at the end of the month.

Let a Program Write Your Checks

With a check-writing program, your computer enters the date automatically. You enter the name of the person or business the check is for, the check amount (only once), and a memo telling what the check is for. The program spells out the check amount on the check, enters the required information in the check register, and calculates the new balance.

This eliminates any discrepancies between what is written on the check and what appears in the register. It also eliminates any errors caused by miscalculations.

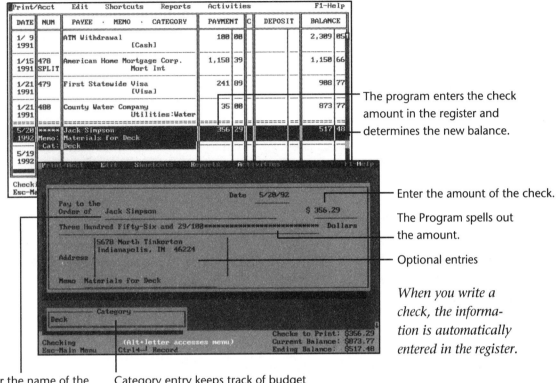

The program enters the check amount in the register and determines the new balance.

Enter the amount of the check.

The Program spells out the amount.

Optional entries

When you write a check, the information is automatically entered in the register.

Enter the name of the person the check is for.

Category entry keeps track of budget information.

By the Way . . .

Printing checks sounds good until you realize everything that's involved. You have to get special checks that fit in your printer, and some printers require that you print a full page of checks (up to 3 checks) at a time. And if you go grocery shopping, you have to tear a check off the page. Many users continue writing checks by hand; they use the check-writing program to record the checks, balance their checkbooks, and manage their budgets.

Balancing the Checkbook in the Old Days

Manually balancing a checkbook can be frustrating. First, you compare your check register to your bank statement, mark each check that has cleared, and make sure the amount of each check as recorded in your register matches the amount on the bank statement.

Next, you total the checks that haven't cleared and add that amount back into your register. Then, you total the deposits that haven't yet been recorded by the bank and subtract that amount from your register. You add up the service charges on the bank statement and subtract them from your register.

Finally, you compare the total in your register with the total on the bank statement, hoping that the two are the same. If you come up with a zero balance, you're done. If not, you must go back to the beginning and compare the amounts of each check to the amounts on the bank statement. You then have to recalculate your balance.

Balancing Your Checkbook in the '90s

With a check-writing program, you simply mark the checks that have cleared, mark the deposits that are recorded on the bank statement, and enter any service charges. The program takes care of the rest, determining the total according to the register.

If the total on your register does not match the total on the bank statement, the program lets you know. You still have to go back and compare the amounts of each check one-by-one. However, if you have to correct an amount, the program automatically recalculates the total in the register, saving you the time of recalculating the balance.

Taking Control of Your Financial Destiny

Before you can take control of your finances, you have to figure out where all your money is going. (Do you really want to know?) For instance, you won't be able to decide if you are spending too much money on auto repair bills unless you know exactly how much you are spending. Would you save money by buying a new car instead? With accurate budget information, you can make a financially sound decision.

With most personal finance programs, you can have the program keep track of each expense for you. Many programs come with a set of home or business expense categories you can use when recording your transactions. If an expense is not listed, you can create your own expense category. Whenever you write a check, you specify the category of the expense. At the end of the month, you tell the program to generate a budget report.

Personal finance programs use *income* and *expense categories* to keep track of money coming in and going out. For example, you may have expense categories for food, clothing, and auto. Most programs allow you to *split a transaction*. For example, if you write a single check for groceries and clothing (you bought a pair of socks at the grocery store), you can assign part of the check to the groceries category and part to the clothing category.

Fancy Finance Features

Check writing and budget reports are the bread and butter of any personal finance program. However, several programs offer additional features that you might find useful:

Recurring entries   If you have a monthly bill that is the same each month (a mortgage payment, rent, or budgeted utility payment), a recurring entry feature can save you time and prevent errors. The program issues the same payment each month.

Bill planning   You enter the information for all the bills you have to pay for the month and then mark the bills you currently plan on paying. The program compares the total amount with your current checking account balance to determine whether you have enough money. You can then prioritize your bills.

Electronic bill paying   If your computer has a modem, you may be able to pay your bills without writing a check. You must subscribe to a service which connects you to your mortgage company, bank, utility company, and others that you have to pay. If you owe money to a person who is not connected to the system, the service will issue them a paper check.

Reminders   A reminder feature will automatically tell you when a bill is due. You specify the number of days in advance you want to be notified. When you start your computer, the program displays a message letting you know if any bills are due.

Income tax estimator   Compare how much you are actually paying in taxes to how much you should be paying to determine whether you are on track for the year.

Investment manager   Now that you have a budget and are saving loads of money, you may decide to invest that money. If you do, an investment manager feature can help you keep track of how your investments are doing.

Financial advice   Some personal finance programs, such as WealthStarter, offer financial advice to help you make such determinations as whether or not you need life insurance and how much you should be saving each month to send Junior to college.

Loan calculator   Some personal finance programs come with a loan calculator that you can use to determine loan payments and figure out just how much interest you will pay. You enter the principal of the loan (how much money you want to borrow), the annual interest rate, and the term; the program figures out the payment, how much goes toward paying off the principal, and how much you pay in interest.

By the Way . . .

If you're in the market for a check-writing program, try Quicken, Quicken for Windows, or Microsoft Money. You should be able to get any of these programs through a mail order company for less than 50 bucks (I saw Money for $30). And if the program saves you from bouncing one or two checks, it can pay for itself.

The Tax Man Cometh

Speaking of personal finances, you can also get programs for doing your taxes. In TurboTax, for example, you enter your name, the amount of money you made, the number of deductions you can claim, and so on; the program determines which forms you need to fill out and how much money the IRS owes you or how much money you owe the IRS. And because all the forms are linked, you enter a piece of information only once; Turbo Tax copies the information to the appropriate forms. For example, you enter your name and social security number only once, and it is placed at the top of every form and schedule.

Popular tax programs include TurboTax, RapidTax, Tax Cut, and Easy Tax. I've done taxes both manually and on a computer, and the computer method is the only way to go.

Keeping Track of Business Income and Expenses

Accounting programs are very similar to personal finance programs—both types of programs help people manage money. However, accounting programs are more sophisticated because they must handle complex business activities including invoicing, inventory control, and payroll.

To handle the complexities of a business, most business accounting programs use a series of interconnected *modules*, as shown on the next page.

With the *invoice module*, you can send invoices to customers to tell the customers how much money they owe you for products or services. The invoice module also helps you keep track of payments received and is linked to the inventory module so that items sold are deducted from inventory.

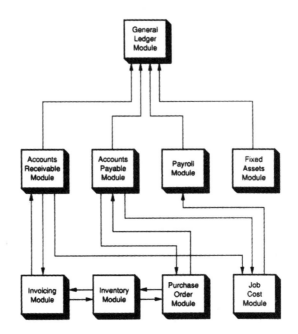

Most accounting programs consist of several modules that interact with one another.

The *fixed assets module* helps keep track of the machines and equipment that your company uses to make money but does not sell to customers, including machinery and computers. The fixed assets module performs depreciation calculations and prepares reports for tax time.

The *job cost module* adds the cost of parts and labor used to produce a product and subtracts it from the amount the product is sold for to determine whether you are making or losing money on a product.

You use the *purchase order module* to order parts or services from vendors or suppliers. When you fill out a purchase order, any products you purchase are recorded in the inventory module, and the cost is deducted from the accounts payable module.

The *payroll module* prepares and prints checks for your employees and prepares quarterly and year-end reports.

The *accounts payable module* keeps track of all the checks you write to vendors for products and services purchased. It also sends necessary information to the job cost module.

Use the *accounts receivable* module to track all incoming money, including payments from customers, and to update balances, past-due payments, and finance charges.

The *general ledger module* acts as a manager, making sure that the information entered in one module gets transferred to all other modules that are affected. For example, say you ship a box of widgets with an invoice to a customer. When you *post* the invoice, the general ledger notifies the inventory module that a certain number of parts were taken out of inventory. In turn, the inventory module notifies the purchase order module that you need to purchase more parts.

> ### By the Way . . .
>
> For business accounting, one of the best programs on the market is PeachTree Accounting. It is both easy to use and powerful. Another popular program is DacEasy. Both programs come with excellent documentation to help you get the program up and running quickly.

Your Personal Secretary: An On-Line Calendar

Most computers have internal, battery-operated clocks that keep track of the date and time. If you ever need to know the current date and time, you can type **date** at the DOS prompt and press **Enter**.

To take full advantage of your computer's date-keeping capacity, however, you should purchase a calendar program (OnTime, The Far Side Calendar, and the Cartoon-A-Day calendar are all popular calendar programs). These programs allow you to plan your schedule and keep track of upcoming dates that are years down the road. You can view the calendars on-screen by year, month, week, or day; print a copy of the calendar; and even have the program remind you of an important appointment.

Keeping the Calendar at Your Fingertips

Most computer calendars run in either of two ways: as *stand-alone* programs or as *memory-resident* programs. As a stand-alone program, a calendar is just like any other calendar—you enter your appointments for each day and then look at the calendar to find out about appointments and things you must do.

In memory-resident mode, the calendar becomes much more powerful. It runs in the background while you work with other programs. If someone calls to make a date, you press a *hot-key* (for example, Ctrl+Alt) for instant access to your calendar. If you turn on the alarm for an appointment, the calendar will beep and display a message to inform you of any upcoming appointment.

Making Appointments: When, Where, and How Long

Before you can take advantage of the computer calendar, you must enter the necessary information for each appointment. In most calendar programs, you enter an appointment by selecting the date and time of the appointment and entering a command to add an appointment to the calendar. The program then displays a dialog box requesting several bits of information.

First, you must enter the amount of time the appointment will last. By entering the length of the appointment, you make sure that you won't run into scheduling conflicts later.

If you want the computer to notify you in advance of upcoming appointments, enter the number of minutes in advance you want to be notified. Keep in mind that the program can notify you only if it is running. If you want the program to notify you of upcoming meetings, be sure to run the program in memory-resident mode. If the program isn't running, it can't do anything.

Most programs also let you specify the *frequency* of the meetings—whether you want this appointment to be monthly, yearly, semiannually, or on some other regular basis. Say you have a scheduling meeting the third Thursday of every month. You enter the appointment on the third Thursday of the current month and the program makes the appointment on every third Thursday of the months to come.

What to Do and When to Do It

To help you remember what you have to do and when, you can use a calendar program to create a To-Do list. You can then repeat the To-Do entry on a regular basis. For example, if you need to balance inventory every month, you can have the entry repeated on a monthly basis.

Put It to Work

When you buy a home or a car, you get a whole new set of responsibilities. With a home, you have a furnace and air conditioner to maintain, a lawn that needs to be fertilized, windows to be washed, and gutters to be cleaned. With a car, there's oil to be changed, brakes to be reshoed, and tires to be rotated. In the hustle and bustle of everyday life, it's easy to forget these things. We put off maintenance until it results in a costly repair.

To help you remember what needs to be done, use a calendar to create a maintenance schedule. You can keep the schedule on the To-Do list, or create recurring appointments on the calendar itself.

The Least You Need to Know

Financial programs and on-line calendars are supposed to make your life easier, not more complicated, so don't get too overwhelmed by all the information in this chapter. Just keep the following information in mind:

- ☛ There are two basic types of money-management programs: personal finance programs and accounting programs.

- ☛ Personal finance programs keep track of income and expenses and help you budget your money as an individual.

- ☛ Accounting programs keep track of bills paid, payments received, inventory, payroll, assets, and other monies in a business.

- ☛ Calendar programs help you keep track of important dates and times, allowing you to print calendars and schedules and view them on-screen.

- ☛ Most calendar programs offer a feature that lets you create a To-Do list to remind you of important projects.

- ☛ You may be able to run the calendar in memory-resident mode. That way, you can quickly switch to the program at any time by pressing a special key, and the program can automatically remind you of upcoming events.

Chapter 17

Give Me the Works: Integrated Software

In This Chapter

- ☞ What integrated software is
- ☞ The pros and cons of integrated software
- ☞ How you can work smarter by using two programs together
- ☞ Popular integrated software packages and what they offer

Integrated software is the Swiss army knife of software packages. In a single package, you usually get a word-processing program, a spreadsheet and/or database program, a communications program (for your modem), and a graphics program (often for one low introductory price). In this chapter, you'll learn whether or not such a program is right for you.

By the Way . . .

The names of integrated programs usually end with the word *Works*: Microsoft Works, Lotus Works, PFS: First Choice. Well, I said *usually*.

Why Go Integrated?

Integrated programs have three basic advantages. First, they are *easy to learn*. All programs in the group have a consistent look and feel, making it easy to learn each program. Once you learn how to print a file in one program, you know how to print a file in all the other programs.

Second, they *work together*. The file formats used in each program are *compatible*, so you can cut and paste data from one file into another. For example, you can cut a picture created in the graphics program and paste it into a letter created in the word-processing program.

Finally (and perhaps most importantly), they are *cheap*. You get several programs for the price of one. You can get any of several integrated packages for under two hundred bucks. Alright, relatively cheap.

Why Not Go Integrated?

Going integrated may not be the best solution for everyone. Integrated packages have a few disadvantages. First, you may not need some of the programs. If you don't need a database or spreadsheet program, why pay for them? If you use only a word-processing program, your money will be better spent on a more advanced word-processing program.

Second, you don't get the advanced features. The several programs you get for the price of one are not the most powerful programs. The word-processing program, for example, usually does not have as many features as one you could purchase separately.

Reaping the Benefits of Integrated Software

Because all the programs in an integrated software package work as a team, you can usually do more with them than you can with individual programs. The following sections show various ways you can use two or more programs together to work smarter.

Pulling Addresses Right Out of Your Address Book

Most integrated packages include a database and a word-processing program. You can create a database to keep the names and addresses of all your relatives, clients, and business contacts.

Although most advanced word-processing programs provide a way to create a database and to merge a database with a document, the database in an integrated program is usually easier to create and work with than the database offered by the word-processing program.

Whenever you need to write a letter to someone whose name is in the database, you can enter codes in the letter that will pull the necessary pieces of information from the database. You then merge the database and letter to place the specified information from the database into the letter. You can use the merge feature to create a single letter or to send letters to as many people listed in the database as desired.

John Smith
123 Main Street
Anycity, CA 92011

Mary Douglas
5555 Emerald Street
Sea Breeze, CA 92540

Joseph Flagenbaum
3 C Avenue, #304
Costa Verde, CA 93092

Database

Dear <First> <Last>,
   Congratulations! The <Last> family has already won $500 cash, a microwave oven, or a cordless telephone. All you need to do is call 1-800-555-1234 to claim your prize.
   Imagine the surprise the residents of <City> will feel when they hear that you have a unique opportunity to take advantage of this vacation resort. Over a thousand other people in the state of <State> have already taken advantage of this offer. Why not call today?

Form letter

Dear John Smith,
   Congratulations! The Smith family has already won $500 cash, a microwave oven, or a cordless telephone. All you need to do is call 1-800-555-1234 to claim your prize.
   Imagine the surprise the residents of Anycity will feel when they hear that you have a unique opportunity to take advantage of this vacation resort. Over a thousand other people in the state of CA have already taken advantage of this offer. Why not call today?

You can merge your address book with a letter to pull information from the address book into the letter.

Plopping Spreadsheets into Your Letters and Reports

If you work with numbers, you can use the spreadsheet to perform all your number crunching for you. If you then need to use the numbers to make a point in a letter or report, you can plop the numbers from the spreadsheet right into your document. Because the spreadsheet works along with the word-processing program, you don't have to worry about reformatting the spreadsheet or printing it on a separate page.

To send a letter by modem, your colleague or friend must have a computer with a modem, and the modem must be turned on and waiting to receive your letter. Or you could send the letter by way of an electronic mail service.

Sending Letters over the Phone Lines

If you have a modem, and the integrated package comes with a communications program, you can create a letter in the word-processing program and send it by way of modem to your colleague or friend.

Have Your PC Place the Call

Some integrated programs have a dialing feature that can dial any phone number displayed on-screen. To use this feature, you must first connect a phone to your modem. (Look back at Chapter 15 for all the messy details about modem communications.)

Use your address book database to find the phone number you want to dial, and then have the telecommunications program dial the number through your modem. When the phone on the other end starts ringing, pick up your phone.

Making Your Point with Graphs

If your integrated program contains both a word-processing program and a graph or charting program, you can create a letter or report in the word processing program and insert a graph anywhere in the document. This is especially useful for sales reports, annual stockholder reports, and other business-related documents.

Saying It Artfully

If your integrated package comes with a collection of clip art and/or a drawing program that lets you create your own art, you can insert art into your documents to create your own customized letterhead, newsletters, and business cards. You can even add small pictures and eye-catching borders to your resume to give it a personal touch.

Popular Integrated Packages and What They Offer

Not all integrated packages are created equal. Some are more like utilities programs that are strong on utilities and weak on everything else. Others contain powerful word-processing and spreadsheet programs, but no database or graphics. The following list provides information about some of the more popular integrated programs:

Microsoft Works for DOS   Includes a word processor with mail merge, a spreadsheet with business graphics, a database manager with report generator, and a telecommunications program. You can work with up to eight files on-screen at once.

Microsoft Works for Windows   The Works for Windows version includes the same programs as the DOS version and offers a drawing program as well. In addition, the program works in Windows, so you can take advantage of the Windows Paint and telecommunications programs.

PFS: First Choice   In addition to the usual programs (word processor, database, spreadsheet, and telecommunications), First Choice offers a graph tool, a calculator, and file management tools that allow you to create directories, and copy, move, and delete files more easily than you could from the DOS prompt. The company that makes this package, Spinnaker, also offers an integrated package for Windows, PFS: WindowWorks.

LotusWorks   Includes the standard programs: word processor, database, spreadsheet, and telecommunications. It also offers a file viewer that lets you view the contents of a file before you open it. LotusWorks features dynamic data linking (DDL). With DDL, you can insert a graph into a document, and whenever you update the graph, the graph that's inside the document is updated.

PC Tools   PC Tools is best known as a utility program (see Chapter 21). However, PC Tools contains an integrated program called Desktop Accessories. The integrated program contains a database, word processor, telecommunications program, a set of calculators, a calendar program, a clipboard (for transferring data between documents), and a macro editor. Although it's not the best integrated program listed here, it may be the best buy of the lot.

By the Way . . .

If you use Microsoft Windows, get Microsoft Works for Windows. It offers the most tools for the money, is easy to learn, and functions the best under Windows. It also features a detailed tutorial to help you learn how to use it.

The Least You Need to Know

Once you know about the individual programs that make up an integrated software package, there's not much more you need to know. That's why this chapter is so short. However, if you are considering purchasing an integrated program, keep the following information in mind:

- ☛ Integrated software offers three major benefits: the individual programs are easy to learn, they work together, and they are inexpensive.

- ☛ Integrated software has two major drawbacks: the package may include programs you won't use, and the individual programs may not be as powerful as a comparable program purchased separately.

- ☛ Integrated software allows you to use two or more programs together to work smarter, faster, and more efficiently.

- ☛ When shopping for an integrated package, compare the programs and tools offered by each package.

Part Three
Guerilla Computing

Somebody should invent a video game that teaches you how to use a computer. At the first level, you would have to enter a computer store and purchase a computer for two thousand dollars. Some salespeople would give you correct information and some would lie just to sell you an obsolete computer. You would have to get out of the store with the best computer your money could buy.

At the next level, you would have to learn how to use common DOS commands to manage your files and to run programs. At this level, you would also get a program and some useless documentation. You would have to learn how to use the program without the documentation.

At the highest level, things would start to go wrong. Your printer wouldn't print. You would enter a command and get a cryptic error message. Your computer would start to gobble up your files, forget it had a hard disk, and format any disk you put in the floppy disk drive. You have to figure out how to get your files back and get your computer back in operation.

I wrote this section as a guide to this imaginary video game. Think of it as your computer survival guide. You will learn how to shop for a computer, how to get by without documentation, what to do when things go wrong, and how to take care of your computer. In short, you will learn how to make it in the computer world without getting eaten alive.

Chapter 18

Shopping for a Computer: How to Spend Lots of Money

In This Chapter

- ☞ Shopping backward: Buying a computer that can run the software you want to use

- ☞ What a microprocessor is, and how you can know if you're getting a good one

- ☞ The amount of memory a computer should have

- ☞ Why you need a hard disk and how big it should be

- ☞ Understanding the different types of floppy disk drives

- ☞ Thinking ahead, so you can prevent your computer from becoming extinct

- ☞ How to select a keyboard, monitor, or printer that's right for you

I've had a lot of computers. I have bought two myself and have had a couple bought for me at work. And I have learned that the only thing certain about computers is that not one of them is the perfect machine. Some don't have the memory it would take to remember their own names. Others are slower than a garden slug in late November. And others don't have the storage space of an overnight bag.

In this chapter, I give you the information you need to avoid some of the mistakes that I (and the people who have bought computers for me) have made in purchasing computers. I prepare you for some of the lingo you'll hear and what it means. And I tell you how to avoid some obsolete equipment.

By the Way . . .

If you are worried that the computer you buy today will become obsolete tomorrow, stop worrying. The computer you buy today is already obsolete. Just make sure it's not overly obsolete. Figure out the system you want, and then plan on spending an additional $500 to get a faster version with more memory and disk space. Buying a computer is a lot like buying a house. You want a computer you can "grow into."

Before You Shop

When you begin shopping for a computer, you need to work backward. Figure out what you want to use the computer for now and what you plan on using it for next year. Think about what software you want to run, what operating system you intend to use, and what other hardware you want to connect to your system. Then, when you are at the store, make sure that each piece of equipment you buy can work with the other pieces and with the software you want to use.

If you plan to run programs written for IBM or compatible computers, you will need an IBM or compatible computer. You cannot run Macintosh software on an IBM PC. You'll learn more about IBM and compatible computers later.

What Software Do You Want to Run?

Evaluating your computer needs may be the most difficult part of the shopping process because you must plan ahead. Although you'll do most of your software shopping after you buy your computer, you must know a few things about the software you intend to use; otherwise, the computer you buy may not be able to run the software.

More Fun Than Cereal Boxes:
Read the Software Packages

When you know what software you want, read the label on the package and make a list of all of the hardware requirements for running each program. Your list might look something like this:

Computer required:	IBM or compatibles
Processor:	80386
Operating system:	MS-DOS or PC DOS 3.2 or higher
RAM required/desired:	512K/640K
Hard disk required:	Yes
Size of disks:	5 1/4"
Graphics required:	Yes
Monitor:	Monochrome, CGA, VGA, and EGA
Mouse required:	Yes

Gimme All the Speed and Power You Got

The microprocessor is the computer's brain. It sets up and controls the communication network that is your computer. Processor names always appear as numbers, such as 80286 or 80386, and are often abbreviated, as in the phrase, "This baby's got a 386 with a 40 meg hard drive!"

The chip number tells you how advanced the microprocessor is. More advanced chips can pass more information along at one time, increasing the speed at which data is shuffled around in the computer. For example, a 286 chip can move only 16 bits of data around at a time. A 386 chip can move 32 bits of data—twice as much.

If you are buying a new computer, don't buy anything less than a 386, and avoid the 386SX variety. SX means that the manufacturer disabled some of the 386 chip's advanced functionality to bring the price down. It also makes the chip slower, and it is not worth the couple hundred bucks you might save.

How Fast Is the Chip?

The speed of the chip is measured in megahertz (pronounced "MEG-a-hurts"). Technically, *hertz* is a unit used to measure the number of times an electronic wave repeats each second. One megahertz is equal to a wave repeating itself one million times in a second.

The *data bus structure* determines how much information the processor can process at one time: 8 bits, 16 bits, or 32 bits. Some chips have an internal and external data bus structure that differs in the number of bits that it can transfer. *Internal* data bus structure refers to how much data the computer can process within the main unit. *External* refers to the amount of data that can be transferred between the main unit and peripherals, such as printers. If you see a computer with two speed listings (for example 16/32MHz), the speeds refer to the internal and external data transfer rates.

Sound fast? With computers, 1 megahertz is a turtle's pace—a slow turtle. Modern computers have speeds in the range of 16 to 76 megahertz, and if you've worked on a 33 megahertz computer, a 16 megahertz computer will seem mighty slow. Don't get anything slower than 20 megahertz, and don't get anything slower than the computer you have at work.

Thanks for the Memory

Your computer uses memory to store program instructions and the data you enter. Some programs require little memory to run and cannot use additional memory even if the computer has it. Most other programs, however, can gobble up as much memory as you give them and still be wanting for more.

The least amount of memory your computer should have is 1 megabyte. If you plan to run Microsoft Windows, the computer should have at least 2 megabytes of RAM. If you plan to run more than one program in Windows, make sure the computer has at least 4 megabytes of RAM. Take any additional RAM if it's offered.

Also, make sure you can add RAM later if needed. With many newer computers, you can install additional RAM in the form of *extended* memory chips and *expanded* memory boards that plug into the motherboard. Although the additional RAM itself may cost more than you want to spend right now, get a computer that will leave the option open for later.

Some computers come with a RAM *cache* (pronounced "cash"). This is a set of fast memory chips that stands between the normal (slower) RAM and the microprocessor. The RAM cache stores frequently used instructions and data, allowing the microprocessor to get the instructions and data more quickly.

Dealers may try to sell a computer with 1M or 2M that does not allow you to add memory later. This is probably an older computer that came equipped with 640K RAM and was expandable *up to* 1M or 2M. The dealer installed the extra RAM to reach the maximum capacity, but the computer is no longer expandable. Make sure you can add RAM to make the total at least 4 megabytes.

A Hard Disk: No Longer an Optional Accessory

To run any of the programs on the market today, you should have a hard disk. A hard disk acts as a permanent storage area for your programs and the data files you create. Most hard disks are housed inside the computer and give the computer instant access to files (you don't have to swap floppy disks into and out of the floppy drives).

How Big is Big Enough?

The size of a hard disk is measured in megabytes (about a million bytes or a million characters). A small hard disk is about 40 megabytes. Large hard disks can be over 500 megabytes.

The size you need depends on the number of programs you want to run, the size of each program, and how much space your data files take up. Read the software boxes to find out how much space you'll need for your programs. Add in the amount of space you'll need for your data. Multiply the total by 4. This will give you a place to start.

By the Way . . .

Don't buy a hard drive that stores less than 80 megabytes, because you will probably regret it later. Many computers come with 40 megabyte hard disks, which can store about 10 programs, if you're lucky. Microsoft Windows requires 6 to 8 megabytes of free space alone, and it is not uncommon to find a program that requires over 10 megabytes.

How Fast Is Fast Enough?

When shopping for a hard disk, don't just focus on the size. Some hard disks are faster than others, and a slow hard disk can slow down your entire system.

Speed is measured in two ways: access time and transfer rate. The *access time* is the average time it takes the drive to move its read/write head to a specified area on the disk. Access time is measured in milliseconds (the lower the number, the faster the drive). Good access times are between 15 ms and 20 ms.

The *transfer rate* is a measure of how much information the drive can transfer from the disk to your computer's memory in a second. A good transfer rate is in the range of 500 to 600 kilobytes per second. (Here, the higher the number, the faster the drive.)

Floppy Disk Drive Size and Capacity

Every computer must have at least one floppy disk drive that allows you to transfer programs and data files from floppy disks to your hard disk. When shopping for a computer, look at the size and capacity of the floppy disk drives.

What Size Disks Can It Take?

IBM computers use both 3 1/2" and 5 1/4" drives (look back at Chapter 4 for more information). Most software used to come on 5 1/4" disks, but more and more companies are packaging their programs on 3 1/2" disks.

If you have the money, get both sizes; an extra floppy disk drive should cost no more than a hundred bucks. If you must choose, choose a 3 1/2" disk drive. If you happen to purchase a program that comes on 5 1/4" disks, you can send to the manufacturer for 3 1/2" disks. Also, make sure the computer has an extra drive bay, so you can install another floppy disk drive later.

High Capacity or Low?

Low-capacity disk drives are a thing of the past. Make sure you get high-capacity drives. A high-capacity disk drive can use both high-capacity and low-capacity disks.

The All-Important Ports

At the back of every system unit are receptacles that allow you to plug in other equipment. A system unit comes with the following standard ports:

What's an FCC Rating? The Federal Communications Commission (FCC) rates computers by two classes, Class A or Class B, which indicate how much radio-frequency interference a computer emits. Class A means that you can safely use the computer in an office. Class B is a stricter rating that means the computer can be used in a home, where the chances of interfering with radios and television sets is greater. If you have a choice, go with Class B.

Make sure your computer has at least two serial ports or a serial port and a mouse port. Otherwise, you will have to use your only serial port for a mouse. If you decide later to connect another serial device (say an external modem), you will have to install another port first.

Parallel printer port   Allows you to connect a parallel printer to the system unit.

Serial or communications port   Allows you to connect a mouse, serial printer, external modem, or other serial device to the system unit.

Monitor port   Allows you to plug your monitor into the system unit.

Keyboard port   Allows you to plug the keyboard into the system unit.

Some computers come with these additional ports:

Game port   Allows you to plug a joystick into the system unit. Many computer games work better with a joystick.

Mouse port   Allows you to connect a mouse to your computer. You can connect the mouse to the mouse port or the serial port.

Planning for Expansion

Once you shell out 2000 bucks for a computer, the last thing you'll want to think about is spending more money to make it better. However, when purchasing a computer, you should think ahead.

When You Need More Than Your Mother: Expansion Boards

Every part of a computer plugs into a big circuit board called the *motherboard*. The motherboard may contain several expansion slots that let you increase the capabilities of your system. You can then plug expansion boards (or cards) into the expansion slots, depending on your requirements. For example, if you buy a program that requires Hercules graphics, you can buy a Hercules graphics card that plugs into your motherboard.

When shopping for a computer, ask the dealer how many *open* expansion slots the computer has, not how many total expansion slots it has. Your computer might have four expansion slots, but those slots may be occupied by video boards (so you can use a monitor), disk drive controller boards (so you can use your floppy or hard drive), or memory boards (for RAM). Make sure the computer has at least four open slots.

How Many Cars Can a Computer Hold? Additional Drive Bays

You also need to think about drive bays. These hold the floppy disk drives that come with your computer. They can also hold useful options that you might want to add later, such as a tape backup unit or a CD-ROM drive. Look for a computer that has three drive bays: one for a 3 1/2" drive, one for a 5 1/4" drive, and one for an optional drive.

Memory Jogger: Adding Memory to Your System

Knowing *that* you can add memory to your computer later is not enough; find out what it takes to add the memory. You should be able to add memory in 1 megabyte units by plugging chips into the motherboard (this costs about 50 bucks per megabyte). If you have to buy a memory board and then add chips, you may end up paying over $100 per megabyte, and the memory usually won't be as fast.

If the system uses something called *proprietary memory*, beware; you'll have to buy the memory chips from the original equipment manufacturer (OEM). This can cost some serious money.

All Keyboards Are Not Created Equal

Although the keys on various keyboards are arranged differently and the number of keys varies, there's not much difference between one keyboard

Recently, I was given a new keyboard at work. The Delete key stuck. In trying to delete a single character, I deleted nearly 1000 of the poor unfortunates. I gave the keyboard back and got a new one that looked like it had a thousand keys. The backspace key was so small it could fit on the head of a pin. It's been two weeks, and I'm finally getting used to it. (I've learned how to avoid the backspace key.) Moral of the story—try before you buy.

and another—all can perform the required tasks. The major distinction between keyboards is the way the keys feel to you. Some keys click when you press them. Some offer little resistance when you press them. And some just feel funny. Buy a keyboard that feels comfortable.

Monitors: Do You Get the Picture?

When you shop for a monitor, pretend you are shopping for a TV. You want the picture to be big and the image to be clear.

There are two types of monitors from which to choose: color or monochrome. Monochrome monitors display a single color against a black or white background, commonly white-on-black or amber-on-black. The amber-on-black configuration is said to be easier on your eyes, but who likes watching a black-and-white TV anyway? Get a color monitor.

Each type of monitor can display a maximum resolution, expressed in dots per inch (dpi). For example, a monitor that offers 640 by 480 dpi resolution contains 640 x 480 dots (or pixels) on its screen. More advanced monitors offer 800 by 600 dpi or 1024 by 768 dpi. In general, the higher the resolution, the sharper the image.

I said "in general" because I have a high-resolution monitor at work on which everything appears a little blurry. My monitor at home is a lower resolution and displays everything very clearly. Don't pay extra for something that doesn't look as good.

A Monitor Isn't Enough

Whenever you purchase a monitor, you must make sure you have a graphics adapter (graphics card) that can control the operation of the monitor and take full advantage of its features. If you have a high-resolution monitor with a low-resolution card, you'll get low resolution. Here's a list of graphics adapters available for color monitors:

CGA (Color Graphics Adapter)   Provides the lowest resolution of the adapters listed. It can display one color in 200 by 640 dpi or four colors in 200 by 320 dpi. If you want to use your computer to play games or create illustrations, don't buy CGA. CGA may also cause eyestrain if you edit on-screen for long periods of time.

EGA (Enhanced Graphics Adapter)   A step up from CGA. It can display 16 colors simultaneously in a resolution of 350 by 640 dpi.

VGA (Video Graphics Array)   Available in three forms: VGA, Enhanced VGA, and Super VGA. VGA displays 256 colors with a resolution of 640 by 480 dpi. Enhanced VGA offers higher resolution: 800 by 600 dpi. Super VGA offers the highest resolution: 1024 by 768 dpi. VGA monitors are excellent for displaying the high-resolution graphics offered in many computer games and graphics programs.

Before you shell out the extra bucks for Super VGA, make sure you need it. Most users and many programs don't take advantage of the increased resolution.

A Page Is Only As Good As the Printer Can Make It

The price of a computer rarely includes the price of a printer, so you'll usually have to purchase the printer separately. Table 18.1 summarizes the pros and cons of each of the five types of printers.

Table 18.1   Choosing the Printer for Your Needs

Printer Type	Advantages	Disadvantages
Dot-matrix	Inexpensive, fast, prints graphics	Poor-quality printing
Daisywheel	High-quality printing	Slow, noisy, expensive, cannot print graphics
Thermal	Lightweight, battery-powered	Slow, poor-quality printing, requires special paper
Inkjet	High-quality printing, prints graphics, quiet	Slow
Plotter	Prints graphics, high-quality printing	Expensive
Laser	Excellent print quality, prints graphics	Expensive

A printer can make or break a computer system. No matter how beautiful documents and graphics look on-screen, if you have a lousy printer, your output is going to look lousy.

CD-ROM: A Warehouse of Information

CD-ROM stands for Compact-Disk Read-Only Memory and is pronounced see-dee-ROM. It is a storage technology that uses the same kind of disks you play in an audio CD player. The disks are made of hard plastic and measure about 4 1/2 inches in diameter. A single disk can store over 600 megabytes of information, which is equivalent to a complete set of encyclopedias.

CDs are best known for their multimedia capabilities. For example, in the National Geographic's Mammals CD, you can read about a cheetah, view a movie clip of cheetahs running and playing, and even listen to the cheetah's eerie purr.

How much will it cost? One of the best CD-ROM deals on the market is the Sony LaserLibrary. For $700 or less, you get all the equipment you need to install the CD-ROM drive on your computer, plus 6 CD-ROM disks that let you use your new toy immediately:

- *Compton's Family Encyclopedia*

- *Microsoft Bookshelf*

- *Languages of the World*

- *National Geographic Mammals*

- *Mixed-Up Mother Goose*

- *World Atlas and Demo*

By the Way . . .

When shopping, consider the access time of the drive—the time it takes to retrieve information from the disk. Drive speeds vary from around 350 milliseconds (.35 seconds) to 1500 milliseconds (1.5 seconds). You will pay more for the faster drive, but the time you save waiting for the computer to access the drive may outweigh the extra expense.

Getting More for Your Buck with IBM Compatibles or Clones

Buying an original IBM computer is like buying vinyl siding from Sears. You pay twice as much for it, but you get a company that stands by its product till the year 3000. Personally, I don't think paying twice as much for an IBM computer or for Sears vinyl siding is worth it, but some people do.

What Are Compatibles and Clones?

IBM compatible computers (sometimes called *clones*) work exactly like IBMs, except that many compatibles are faster, cost less, and use higher quality parts than their IBM counterparts. You may have heard of some of the better known IBM compatible computers, including Compaq, AST Premium, Dell Computers, Northgate, ALR, Zenith, Hyundai, Everex, Epson, and Gateway.

The word *clone* is a derogatory term describing a compatible computer assembled by a local computer dealer. Clone computers have the same status as generic food—they cost less, but may not offer the same quality as the name-brand compatibles. I say *may not* because some clones are actually superior to their name-brand counterparts.

Living Together: Hardware and Software Compatibility

Compatibility refers to both hardware and software. Software compatibility means you can run IBM software on the compatible computer without any problems. Hardware compatibility means you can use IBM parts to repair and upgrade your compatible.

Software Included?

Some dealers include the cost of the operating system in the price they quote you; others don't. You can't run the computer without one. If the computer does include an operating system, make sure it includes the documentation you need to learn the system.

Some dealers may also offer free applications with a computer. For example, many computers now come equipped with Microsoft Windows 3.1. When you're comparing prices, consider the software included.

The Least You Need to Know

Okay, I admit it, this is way too much information to remember when you go to the local computer store. To help, I have included a card that you can Xerox and take to the store with you. Shop around, fill out the forms, and then come back to this chapter. Also, here are some quick shopping guidelines:

- ☞ Get a computer with at least an 80386 processor chip.

- ☞ SX stands for "stinks." If somebody tries to sell you a 386SX computer, leave.

- ☞ Don't buy a genuine IBM computer. With an IBM compatible, you can usually get twice as much for half the money.

- ☞ Get a computer with at least 2 megabytes of RAM, 4 megabytes if you want to run Windows. Make sure you can add RAM up to 16 megabytes without having to add a memory board.

- ☞ Get a computer with a hard disk drive that can store up to 80 megabytes.

- ☞ Make sure the floppy disk drive is a high-density drive.

- ☞ Try out the keyboard to make sure it feels right. If it doesn't, make a deal to get a different keyboard.

- ☞ Get a VGA monitor or better.

- ☞ If the computer doesn't come with a mouse, ask why not. Then browbeat the salesperson to give you one for free.

- ☞ Service agreements are a rip-off. The computer should come with a guarantee. If it doesn't work, it's their fault, not yours.

- ☞ Don't trust computer ads or sales pitches; if an ad sounds too good to be true, it probably is.

Chapter 19
Surviving Without Documentation

In This Chapter

- ☞ How to print a list of files
- ☞ How to install a program on a hard disk
- ☞ Reading a list of files to figure out how to run a program
- ☞ How to display the contents of a help file on-screen
- ☞ How to run a Windows program
- ☞ How to get around in most programs
- ☞ Common ways to get help in a program

Worst case scenario—you get a program, and there's no documentation. None of your friends know how to use the program, and the local bookstore doesn't have a book about this program. What do you do? The following sections provide some tactics for dealing with such situations. Although they won't work for all programs, they will work for most.

Every suggestion in this chapter is built on common sense. You are merely looking for ways to find help, just as you look for help when you are lost; you try to find a person who has an intelligent face or you look for a familiar landmark. Don't be afraid to try these various tactics. You won't hurt anything, and you will probably learn a great deal.

Gathering Clues: Print a List of Program Files

To solve any mystery, you must first gather clues. In this case, the clues are the names of the files that make up the program, and these names can tell you a lot. So the first thing you should do is print out the list of file names:

Step 1: If you just got the program, write-protect the first disk in the set, stick it in one of the floppy disk drives, and close the drive door. Change to the drive that contains the disk. If the program is already installed on the hard disk, change to the drive and directory where the program files are stored.

> ### By the Way . . .
> If you forgot how to write-protect a disk, here's a brief review. For 3 1/2" disks, slide the write-protect tab so you can see through the hole. For 5 1/4" disks, tape over the write-protect notch on the side of the disk. (Use a piece of masking tape if you don't have a bona fide write-protect sticker.)

Step 2: Make sure your printer is turned on.

Step 3: Type **dir > prn** and press **Enter**. DOS prints a directory listing containing the names of all files in the current drive and directory. Here's an example:

Volume in drive B is GWS
Volume Serial Number is 12EB-2009
Directory of B:

GWS	EXE	176410	04-29-92	2:18p
GWS	DOC	129796	11-07-91	3:28p
GWSINSTL	EXE	37458	11-07-91	11:31a
GWSDRV	RES	107225	11-07-91	2:39p
GWSPDR	RES	32044	08-11-91	6:08p
GWS	RES	143239	11-07-91	3:35p
EXAMPLE2	GIF	24576	01-01-80	3:36a

EXAMPLE3	GIF	27878	08-25-91	10:52a
RMOVER	EXE	19034	09-08-91	3:00p
EXAMPLE1	IMG	62630	08-28-91	3:00p
GWSSCN	RES	10523	09-05-91	10:07p
README	DOC	17643	11-01-91	9:30a
VIEW-ME	IMG	21041	12-20-90	6:48p

        12 file(s) 809497 bytes
                 662528 bytes free

Bingo! A SETUP or INSTALL File

Programs commonly come with their own setup or installation programs. You run the program, and it automatically creates a directory on your hard drive, decompresses the files (if necessary), and copies them to the new directory. You may have to answer a few questions.

If you see a file called SETUP.BAT, SETUP.COM, SETUP.EXE, INSTALL.BAT, INSTALL.COM, INSTALL.EXE, or a similar name, type the name of the file without its extension, and press Enter. For example, type **install** and press **Enter**. Follow the on-screen instructions to proceed.

Ready to Run? You're in Luck

Some programs come ready to run. To install the program on your hard disk, you copy the files from the program disks to a directory on your hard disk. To learn how to create directories, change to a directory, and copy files, refer to Chapter 7. In other cases, the operation may be more complex, as you will see next.

Look for a File with ZIP

Many programs come with their files *compressed*, so they take up less disk space and fewer disks. If you display a directory of a program disk and see only one or two file names, it is likely that the program files are compressed into a single file.

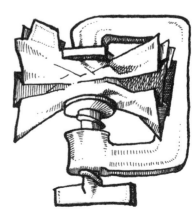

If PKUNZIP.EXE is not on the disk, you can get a copy by calling PKWARE, Inc. at (414) 354-8699. You might also be able to get a copy to try for free from a local computer user group or a computer store. Because PKZip is a *shareware* product, you can try the product for free, and then send money to PKWARE if you decide to continue using the product.

A common program used to compress files is PKZIP. PKZIP works in either of two ways: it creates a ZIP file (a file with the extension .ZIP) that contains all the program files in a compressed format, or it creates a file with the .EXE extension that decompresses the files automatically (this is called a *self-extracting* ZIP file). The method for decompressing files depends on the method used to compress the files.

Decompressing a ZIP File

To decompress a ZIP file, first copy the ZIP file and the file PKUNZIP.EXE to a directory on your hard disk. Change to the drive and directory that contains the ZIP file. Type **pkunzip** *filename*.**zip** (where *filename* is the name of the zipped file) and press **Enter**. PKUNZIP decompresses the file. Delete the ZIP file from your hard disk, so it doesn't take up disk space.

Decompressing an .EXE File

An .EXE file is a program file, so you can run it as you would run any program. First, copy the .EXE file to a directory on your hard disk. Change to the drive and directory that contains the file. Type the .EXE file's name without the .EXE extension and press **Enter**. The files are decompressed in the current directory. Delete the .EXE file from your hard disk.

How can you tell if the .EXE file is a zipped file? You can't until you try to run it. If you run it, and it shows on-screen that it is unzipping itself, you just hit pay dirt. If not, you haven't hurt anything. Give it a shot.

By the Way . . .

PKZip is one of the most popular compression programs on the market, but it's not the only one. A different compression program may have been used.

Look for a README File

Some programs come with a file called README that often contains information about installing and running the program, details about how the program works, information about new features, or a name and address where you can send to get more complete documentation.

Running a README File

If you find a file called README.BAT, README.COM, README.EXE or a similar name with the extension .BAT, .COM, or .EXE, you can run the README file as you can run any program file. To run such a README file, type its name at the DOS prompt (without the extension .BAT, .EXE, or .COM) and press **Enter**. The program will then display the information for you.

Viewing a README File

If you find a README text file (a file with the extension .DOC or .TXT, or a file named READ.ME), you must enter a DOS command to display the contents of the file on-screen. To view the file's contents, take the following steps:

An easier way to view the contents of the README file is to print the file. Type the following command and press **Enter**. (Remember to substitute the actual file's name in place of *readme.txt*.)

copy readme.txt > prn

Step 1: Change to the disk and directory that contains the README file. (The name of the README file may vary. It is commonly called README.TXT or README.DOC.)

Step 2: Type **type readme.txt | more** where *type* tells DOS to display the contents of the file on-screen, *readme.txt* is the name of the README file, and | *more* tells DOS to pause after displaying each screenful of information.

Step 3: Press **Enter**. DOS displays the first screenful of information.

Step 4: Read the information and then press **Enter** to see the next screen.

Step 5: Repeat step 3 until you are returned to the DOS prompt.

Look for Files That End in .BAT, .COM, or .EXE

A README file is nice, but it's not essential—you can usually get along without it. Keep in mind that your first goal is to learn how to run the program, and that the three types of files that run a program have names that end in .BAT, COM, and .EXE. So go back to your list of file names and mark all the files that end in .BAT, .COM, or .EXE.

Narrow Down the List

Now you can start narrowing down the list. First, look for .BAT files. They typically contain commands that run the correct .COM or .EXE file along with any *switches* to tell the .COM or .EXE files exactly how to run. If a batch file is included, it's a good clue that typing the name of an .EXE or .COM file either will not work or will not work the best.

Mark any batch file whose name appears to represent the program's name. For example, say you have a program called BlackDoom; look for names such as BD.BAT, BLACK.BAT, or BDOOM.BAT. Do the same for file names that end in .COM and .EXE.

Now you can try running the program. Use each promising file name from most promising to least promising (.BAT files first, .COM second, and .EXE third) until you hit on the right one.

To run a program, first change to the drive and directory that contains the program files. Type the first part of the program file's name (omit the period and the extension). For example, to run Microsoft Windows, you would type **win** without the period and without *exe*. Press **Enter**. If the program started, you're all set. Keep trying program names until you hit on the right one.

It Might Be a Windows Program

You cannot run a Microsoft Windows program from the DOS prompt. If you cannot get a program to run or you get a message saying that this program requires Windows, try running the program from Windows.

To run a program from Windows, first start Windows at the DOS prompt (type **win** and press **Enter**). Click on File in the Program Manager's pull-down menu bar and select **R**un. Type a complete path to the drive and directory in which the program's files are stored followed by the name of the file that executes the program. For example, type **c:\graph\graph.exe**. Press **Enter** or click on **OK**.

The Program Is Running, Now What?

Once you have a program up and running, your next concern is how to get around in the program. The technique for navigating in the program will vary depending on whether the program is *command-driven* or *menu-driven*. With command-driven programs, each command corresponds to a function key or a key combination, such as F5 or Ctrl+F1 or Shift+F3. You have to know which key to press. With menu-driven programs, you can select commands from a pull-down menu at the top of the screen or by using some other menu system.

Menu-Driven? A Piece of Cake

If you start a program and a menu appears on-screen, you're in luck. To enter commands, you simply open a menu and select the command. You have only one initial problem—how to open a menu. Here are some techniques that work in a wide range of programs:

Look for a message. Look at the top or bottom of the screen for a message such as **Press Alt for menus** or **Right-click for menus**. Follow the messages.

Try the Alt key. In most programs (including all Windows programs), you can activate a menu by pressing Alt plus the highlighted letter or first letter in the menu's name. If that doesn't work, try pressing the **Esc** (Escape) key, the **Ctrl** key, or the **F10** key.

Try the mouse. Move the mouse pointer to the top of the screen and click the left mouse button, the right mouse button, or both buttons. Some menus are like roaches—you never know where they are and what it will take to get them out of hiding.

Try another menu. Once a menu is open, you can usually switch to the menu on the left or right by using the left and right arrow keys.

Choose an item. To choose an item from a menu, click on the item, type the highlighted letter in the item's name, or use the arrow keys to highlight it and press **Enter**.

Check out the submenus. If the item you choose is followed by an arrow, a submenu will appear, and you will have to make another choice. If the item is followed by two or three dots (..), a dialog box may appear, requesting additional information.

Look Again at the Screen

You'll often be surprised at the number of problems and mysteries you can solve by taking a step back and looking carefully at the screen. Many programs display a function key bar at the bottom of the screen that shows the commands you can enter. Simply press a function key to enter the designated command.

Other programs display a status line at the bottom of the screen that contains messages about what you can do next. For example, you might see the message **READY**, meaning you can start working. Or the message may tell you which key you need to press in order to display the Help screen.

F1—Computing's 911

Just as 911 is a standard phone number to call in case of emergencies, the F1 key is used by most programs to display a help screen. Try pressing **F1** and see what happens. Many programs will display a Help index that lists help with keystrokes. If this choice is available, choose it to find out which keys you need to press to enter commands.

If the Help screen contains a Print command, select this command to print the information you need. If a Print command is not available, make sure the help you need is displayed on-screen, make sure your printer is on, and then press the **Print Screen** key. This sends everything on-screen to your printer. It's a messy way to print, but it gets you what you need.

A Built-In Tutor? You've Struck Gold

Some programs come with a tutorial that leads you through the process of using the program's major features. Display a directory of the program's files and look for a file such as TUTOR.EXE, TUTOR.COM, LEARN.EXE, or LEARN.COM. If you find such a file, try running it.

When All Else Fails

Okay, so you've tried everything and the screen still gives you a blank stare. Don't give up yet. Here are some final words of wisdom from our resident hacker, Faithe Wempen:

Watch the screen and press each function key. Observe what each function key does, and take notes. Try each function key alone, then hold down the **Shift** key while pressing each function key. Hold down the **Alt** key and press each function key. Finally, hold down the **Ctrl** key and press each function key.

Try the other keys. If the function keys don't work, try the other keys. Start with the number keys, then the letter keys, each separately and then in conjunction with the Alt, Ctrl, and/or Shift keys until you find something that changes the screen in some way.

Click or click and hold the left mouse button on an item. Many times, this will give you an explanation of the item or will call up a menu. If that doesn't work, try the right mouse button.

Press the Esc key. A menu or message might appear telling you what to do next.

To exit, press Esc, Ctrl+Esc, or Ctrl+Break. If none of these keys works, perform a warm boot as a last resort by pressing **Ctrl+Alt+Del.**

The Least You Need to Know

As you get more accustomed to using a computer, you'll be more and more tempted to try using each program without looking at the documentation. As you take on greater and greater challenges, keep the basics in mind:

☞ If you don't have documentation for a program, the first thing you should do is view a directory of the program's files.

☞ If you see a file called SETUP or INSTALL, type the file name (without the period or extension) at the DOS prompt and press **Enter**. The program will install itself.

☞ Program files are commonly compressed into one file. If you see a file that has the .ZIP extension, you can use PKUNZIP to decompress the program files.

☞ Some programs contain a README file or other text file that may contain instructions on how to install and use the program. Some README files contain only update information or fixes for common problems.

☞ Program files whose names end in .BAT, .COM, or .EXE are files that might execute the program. To run one of these files, type its name (without the period or extension) at the DOS prompt and press **Enter**.

☞ If the program is a Microsoft Windows program, you must run it from Windows.

☞ Some programs contain a menu or pull-down menu bar that you can use to enter commands. To activate the menu bar, try the Alt key or the mouse.

☞ A common way to get help in a program is to press the **F1** key.

Chapter 20

"I've Fallen and I Can't Get Up": Some Trouble-shooting Tips

In This Chapter

- ☞ What to do in a crisis, and what not to do
- ☞ How to find the cause of a problem
- ☞ What to do when your computer won't boot
- ☞ Why your program won't run, and how you can fix it
- ☞ How to scare a mouse pointer out of hiding
- ☞ What to do when your mouse pointer jumps around the screen
- ☞ Common reasons why a modem won't work
- ☞ Why your computer will refuse to read a disk
- ☞ What might cause your keyboard to flip out or die
- ☞ Common printer problems, and how to solve them
- ☞ How to make your computer work faster

Computers are fickle. You might use your computer all week without a problem. Then, on Friday, you try to run a program you've been using all week, and the following message appears on-screen:

Bad command or filename

Or you try to print a file, and the file won't print. The printer is on, it has paper in it, and everything else seems to be okay. But no matter what you do, the printer won't print the file.

What should you do? In this chapter, you will learn how to react in a crisis and how to solve your own computer woes. Although I can't cover every problem in this chapter, I will cover many common problems to give you a taste of the types of things that can go wrong.

Troubleshooting Tactics: Solving Your Own Problems

With a little patience, you can solve your own problems. You just have to know how to go about it—what to do and what not to do. The overall tactic is twofold: you need to trace the problem back to its cause and not make the problem worse than it already is.

When you run into a problem that doesn't have an obvious solution, the best course of action is inaction; that is, don't do anything. If you're fidgety to do something, take a walk or wash the dishes until you're no longer in a panic. Then come back and try some of the following tactics.

Look for Clues

The answer to most problems is probably staring you in the face. So, the first thing you should do is look at the monitor for any messages that indicate a problem. Although on-screen messages are usually very general, they provide a starting point. If you don't see anything on-screen, start asking yourself some questions.

When did the problem start? Think back to what you did before the problem arose. Did you install a new software program? Did you enter a command? Did the computer freeze up? Knowing when the problem started can often reveal the cause.

Is the problem limited to one program? If you have the same problem in every program, the problem is probably caused by your computer. If the problem occurs in only one program, it is probably caused by the program.

Is everything plugged in and turned on? If a part of your computer is dead—no lights, no sound, no action, it probably isn't connected or isn't turned on. Turn everything off and check the connections. Don't assume that just because something looks connected it is; wiggle the plugs.

When did you have the file last? If you lost a file, it probably did not get sucked into a black hole. It is probably somewhere on your disk, in a separate directory. Try to think back to when you had the file last and to what directory you saved it to.

> ## By the Way . . .
> Don't overlook the obvious. Many problems have quick solutions. The printer may not be turned on, a cable may be disconnected, or you may be looking for a file in the wrong directory. You may need to look away from the problem in order to see it.

It's Probably Not the Computer

Most novice computer users (and some experienced users) automatically assume that whenever a problem arises, the computer is on the blink. Although the computer itself can be the cause of some major problems, it is rarely the cause of minor, everyday problems. The problem is usually in the software: DOS, Windows, or one of your applications.

My Computer Won't Boot

A computer is a lot like a car; the most frustrating thing that can happen is that you can't even get the engine to turn over. To solve the problem, consider these questions.

Is the computer on? Are the lights on the computer lit? If so, the computer is plugged in and is on. If not, check to make sure the computer is plugged into an outlet, that your power strip (if you use one) is on, and that the other end of the computer plug is plugged securely into the computer. Finally, make sure the power switch on the system unit is turned on.

Is the screen completely blank? Even though the screen is completely blank, the computer may have booted; you just can't see it. If you heard the computer beep and you saw the drive lights go on and off, the computer probably booted fine. Make sure the monitor is turned on and the brightness controls are turned up. If that doesn't work, turn everything off and then check to make sure the monitor is plugged securely into the system unit.

OOPS!

To create a bootable floppy disk, get a blank disk for drive A (not drive B). Insert the disk in drive A, type **format a: /s**, and press **Enter**. When DOS is done formatting the disk, you have a bootable floppy disk. Put it in drive A, close the drive door, and press **Ctrl+Alt+Del** to see if the disk works. If it doesn't work, remove the disk, press **Ctrl+Alt+Del**, and yell for help.

Is there a disk in drive A? If you see a message on-screen that says **Non-system disk or disk error**, you probably left a floppy disk in drive A. Remove the disk and press any key to boot from the hard disk.

Can you boot from a floppy disk? If you still can't get your computer to boot from the hard disk, try booting from a bootable floppy disk. Insert the bootable floppy disk in drive A, close the drive door, and press **Ctrl+Alt+Del**. If you can boot from a floppy, the problem is on your hard disk. You'll need some expert help to get out of this mess.

My Screen Is Flickering

If your screen is flickering or turning odd colors, the plug that connects the monitor to the system unit has probably come loose. Turn everything off, and then check the connection. If the plug has screws that secure it to the system unit, tighten the screws.

By the Way . . .

One day, I noticed the left side of my monitor turning purple and green, sort of like a mood ring. I thought the monitor had gone south. Problem was, I had set a speaker next to the monitor, so I could hear the nifty sounds from a new toy I acquired. Apparently, the magnet in the speaker was turning my screen funny colors. I moved the speakers, turned everything off for the night, and the next morning things were back to normal.

I Can't Get the Program to Run

You got a new program, installed it, and entered the command to run the program. The following message appears on-screen: **Bad command or file name**. What's wrong?

Are you in the drive and directory where the program's files are stored? Some programs install themselves and set up your system so you can run the program from any drive or directory. With other programs, you must change to the drive and directory that contains the program's files in order to run the program.

Did you type the correct command? The command must be typed exactly as specified in the documentation. If you mistype the command, the program won't run. If you don't have the documentation, refer to Chapter 19 to figure out what to do.

Did you install the program correctly? Installing some programs consists of merely copying the program's files to a directory on your hard disk. With other programs, you must run an installation program. If the program requires you to run an installation program, and you did not, the program probably won't run.

Is it a Windows program? You cannot run a Windows program from the DOS prompt. Run Windows first, and then try running the program.

(See Chapter 8.) Or, try typing **win** followed by the command required to run the program, and then press **Enter**. For example, type **win excel** and press **Enter**.

I Have a Mouse, but I Can't Find the Pointer On-Screen

Once you get your mouse working, you will probably never have to mess with it again. The hard part is getting the mouse to work in the first place. If you connected a mouse to your computer and you don't see the mouse pointer on-screen, there are a few possibilities you should investigate.

Are you in a program that uses a mouse? Some programs don't *support* a mouse, so you won't see the mouse pointer in these programs. For example, you won't see a mouse pointer at the DOS prompt, but you should see one in the DOS Shell. Run a program that you know uses a mouse.

Is the mouse pointer hidden? Mouse pointers like to hide in the corners or edges of your screen. Roll the mouse on your desktop to see if you can bring the pointer into view.

Is the mouse plugged securely into your system unit? Turn everything off and then make sure that your mouse is securely connected to the system unit. The plug may be loose. Restart your system.

When you connected the mouse, did you install a mouse program? Connecting a mouse to your computer is not enough. You must install a program (called a *mouse driver*) that tells the computer how to use the mouse. Follow the instructions that came with the mouse to figure out how to install the program.

When you installed the mouse program, did you specify a COM port? When you install a mouse program, the program may ask you if the mouse is connected to COM1, COM2, or COM3, the serial ports on your computer. Give the wrong answer, and your computer won't be able to find your mouse. Run the installation or setup program again and select a different COM port. Reboot after each change, and write down every change you made.

> **By the Way . . .**
>
> Speaking of writing down every change you make, it's a good idea to always write down any changes you make to your system. Although it takes a little extra time, it allows you to retrace your tracks later.

My Mouse Pointer Is Jumpy

If your mouse pointer jumps around the screen rather than moving smoothly, your mouse may have fur balls. To find out what these fur balls are and how to get rid of them, look ahead to Chapter 21.

I Can't Get My Modem to Work

Funny, I can't get mine to work either. I mean, I can't get Prodigy to find my modem when I run Prodigy from Windows. It works fine from DOS, and my Windows telecommunications program works fine. I could do it on my old computer, and I can do it at home, but when I changed computers at work, some evil wizard must have messed with things. Maybe by the next edition of this book, I'll have the problem resolved. As for your problem, ask yourself a few questions.

Is the modem plugged in and turned on? If you have an external modem, it must be plugged into a power source, to the system unit, and to a phone line. Make sure all the connections are secure, and that the modem's power switch is on. If you have an internal modem, make sure it is connected to a phone jack.

Is the phone working? You can check a phone jack by plugging a regular phone into the jack. Lift the phone off the hook and listen for a dial tone. If you don't hear a dial tone, the jack is dead, and your modem won't be able to dial out.

TECHNO NERD TEACHES

Each port on a computer is assigned an *address* and an *interrupt*. The address tells the computer where the port is located. The interrupt is a code that tells the computer which port is requesting attention from the computer. If you install a modem, and it is set up to use an address or interrupt that is already being used by another device, the two devices will confuse your system. To prevent conflicts, expansion cards (such as internal modems) have a set of switches that allow you to change the address and interrupt. You may also have to change it in your programs. This is a job for Mr. Wizard; don't mess with interrupts unless you know what you're doing.

Am I dialing the wrong number? Silly question, but it's a common cause. If you hear an angry voice coming out of the modem, you probably woke somebody up. Hopefully they don't have Caller ID. Also, if you normally have to dial a number before dialing out (say 9), type the number, a comma, and then the phone number.

Do I have pulse or tone service? Pick up your phone and dial a few numbers. If you hear clicks, you have pulse (or rotary) service, even if you have a phone with buttons. If you hear beeps, you have tone service. If your telecommunications program is set for tone service, and you have rotary service, it won't be able to dial out. Try resetting your telecommunications program for rotary service; it's usually as easy as checking an option box.

Does my program know where the modem is? Most computers have two COM ports. Usually, a mouse is connected to COM1, and COM2 is left open for another device, often a modem. Your communications program or on-line service program allows you to specify the COM port being used by your modem. Try changing the COM port setting.

Are my communications settings correct? If your communications program can find your modem, dial a number, and establish a connection, but can do nothing else, your communications settings are probably incorrect. If your baud setting is 9600 bps or higher, try changing it to 2400. Then check the other settings, as explained in Chapter 15.

The Computer Won't Read My Floppy Disk

Don't feel bad, it happens to everyone. You stick a floppy disk in the disk drive, close the drive door, change to the drive, and you get an error message saying basically that the disk is no good. DOS can't read it or write to it or even see that it's there. What happened? That depends.

Is the disk inserted properly? Even the most experienced computer user occasionally inserts a disk upside-down or sideways into the disk drive. (I've even inserted a disk in the slot between the disk drives!) Check to make sure the disk is in the right slot the right way.

Is the disk drive door closed? If the drive has a door, it must be closed. Otherwise, you'll get an error message saying that DOS can't read or write to the disk.

If a disk is bad, you may be able to salvage it using a utility program, as explained in the next chapter. If a drive is bad, you'll have to take it to a computer mechanic and get it fixed. Usually the problem is that the drive is not spinning at the right speed or that the arm that reads and writes data to the disk is not aligned properly on the disk.

Is the disk write-protected? If the disk is write-protected, you won't be able to save a file to the disk.

Is the disk full? If you try to save a file to a disk and you get an **Insufficient space** message, the disk has insufficient free space to hold any more data. Use a different disk.

Is the disk formatted? If you buy new, unformatted disks, you must format the disks before you can use them.

Did you format the disk to the proper density? If you format a high-density disk as a low-density disk, or vice versa, you will probably run into problems when you try to use the disk.

Is the disk bad? Although it's rare, disks do go bad. Some disks even come bad from the manufacturer. If you get a **Sector not found** or **Data error** message, the disk may be bad. Then again, the drive might need a tune-up. Try some other disks. If you're having problems with all disks, the problem is in the drive. If you are having trouble with only one disk, it's the disk.

Everything I Type Is in Capital Letters!

If everything you type comes out uppercase, you have probably pressed the Caps Lock key by mistake. Press it again to turn Caps Lock off. Most keyboards have an indicator light that shows when Caps Lock is on. Likewise, some programs will display a message, such as **CL**, at the bottom of the screen when Caps Lock is on.

I Can't Move Down with the Down Arrow Key

In most word-processing programs, you can't move down with the down arrow key until you have some text to move down to. You need to type some text or press the **Enter** key to move down. Once you have some text and paragraphs on-screen, you can move up or down with the arrow keys.

My Keyboard Is Schizophrenic

Some fancy keyboards allow you to *remap* the keys. For example, you can make the F1 key on the left side of the keyboard act like the Enter key, or you can make it perform a series of keystrokes. Advanced users like to remap keys to customize the keyboard and make it a real time-saver.

However, if you accidentally press the remap key and then continue typing, you may remap your entire keyboard without knowing it. You'll know it when you press the K key and get a Z or you press the Spacebar and delete a paragraph. You can usually unmap the keyboard. If you have an AnyKey keyboard, try this:

First: Press **Ctrl+Alt+Suspend Macro** to stop remapping your keyboard and make it normal again.

If that doesn't work: You may have remapped your Ctrl or Alt key. Press the **Remap** key, press **Ctrl** twice, press **Alt** twice, and press **Remap** again. Then try **Ctrl+Alt+Suspend Macro** again.

If you don't have an AnyKey keyboard, I can't help you. Get out the handy-dandy documentation that came with your computer and try to find something about remapping the keys.

My Keys Stick

If you have an old keyboard, or if you spilled something on the keyboard, the keys might start to stick. Take the keyboard to a computer service and have it cleaned. Or buy a new keyboard.

My Keyboard Is Completely Dead

If your keyboard is completely dead, or if your computer displays the message **Keyboard not found** when you boot your computer, do a quick inspection.

Is the keyboard plugged in? Turn off the computer, and then check the connection. Don't just look at it—wiggle the plug. Reboot the computer.

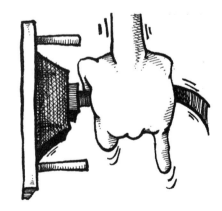

Is the other end of the cable connected? Turn off the computer and check the connection at the keyboard. Some keyboards come with a cable that's permanently attached. Others have a little connector that can come loose.

Is the keyboard cable bent or frayed? Check the condition of the keyboard cable. If it is bent or frayed, purchase a new cable.

My File Is Gone

Files are like shoes; they rarely disappear forever, but they do get misplaced. If you think a file is gone, don't panic; you have probably just misplaced it. Try these rescue techniques.

If you accidentally deleted a file, it is gone. If you know that you deleted a file, the file is gone, not just misplaced. However, you might be able to get it back. Change to the drive and directory where the deleted file was, type **undelete *.*** and press **Enter**. If you have DOS version 5 or later, you'll see a list of files you can undelete. Press **Y** for each file you want to undelete. If this doesn't get the file back, you may need to use a utility program, as explained in the next chapter.

Look in the program's default directory. Many programs have a default directory where they save any files you create and save. Unless you specify otherwise, all files are saved to this directory. Check the directory that contains the program files for your data file.

Many utility programs come with a file finder. You tell the program to find a file, specify the file's name, and then unleash the file finder. It will sniff out a file better than a Georgia bloodhound.

If you know the file's name, have DOS find it. If you know the file's exact name, type this command at the DOS prompt: **dir \filename.ext /s** (where *filename.ext* is the name of the file) and press **Enter**. DOS will search the entire disk drive for the file and show you the directory where the file is stored. If you have more than one hard drive, the file may be on a different drive. Repeat this command for each disk drive.

If you don't know the file's name, use wild cards. If you don't know the file's name, you can use wild-card characters in place of any characters you can't remember. For example, to find all files that have the .DOC extension, you could enter **dir *.doc /s** at the DOS prompt. Add the /P switch to keep the file list from scrolling off-screen. For example, type **dir *.doc /s /p** and press **Enter**.

My Printer Won't Print

Printers are a pain. They're a pain to set up and a pain to use. And even if you get the printer to finally work with one program, there is no guarantee that it will work with the next one. So, if you're running into printer problems, you will probably have to do more fiddling than Nero. Here are some things to look for:

Check the connections. Turn off the computer and printer, and make sure the printer is securely connected to the printer port on the system unit and to a power supply. Make sure the power supply (a power strip, for instance) is turned on. Make sure the printer is turned on.

Does the printer have paper? A printer will refuse to print without paper, but most printers won't tell you that they're out of paper. Check the paper supply and make sure the paper is feeding correctly into the printer.

Try the Load/Eject button. Some printers have a Load button that you must press to get paper to start feeding into the printer. You press the button only once—to start the paper feeding. The printer takes it from there.

Is the on-line light lit? If the on-line light is off or is flashing, the printer is not ready to print. Try pressing the on-line button (if the printer has one) or the **Reset** button.

Do you have trouble printing in only one program? If you can print problem-free in another program, you may have selected the wrong printer in the program that's giving you problems. Read the documentation that came with the program to figure out how to set up a printer. Then check your printer setup in the program. Also, check to make sure you selected the right printer port (usually LPT1). If you have a program you can print in, check its printer setup and model the new printer setup after it.

Check the print queue. Many programs print a file to a *print queue* on disk; the queue (or print manager) then feeds the file to the printer. The print queue may stop sending information to the printer for a variety of reasons (usually because the printer is off or not on-line). You need to do two things:

Get the printer on and on-line. Until the printer is ready to accept information, the print queue will not send the file.

Tell the print queue to start or continue the print job. This process will vary from program to program. In Windows, for example, you can press **Ctrl+Esc** and choose **Print Manager** from the list of programs. The Print Manager window appears, showing which files are currently in the queue. You can then enter a command to continue the print job.

My Computer Seems Slower Than Normal

Computers can seem sluggish for a number of reasons.

You are running Microsoft Windows. Microsoft Windows, and other graphic interfaces, require a lot of computer power. It's normal for your computer to run more slowly when running such a program. There are ways to speed up Windows, which usually consist of shrinking the windows you don't need and clearing as much stuff off the screen as possible. There are other ways beyond the scope of this book. For help with Windows problems, try *Windows Woes*, by a guy named Paul McFedries.

Somebody pressed your Turbo switch. Some computers have a Turbo switch that makes the computer run faster. (Why would you want it to run more slowly? Maybe so you could catch more lemmings.) With some computers, the Turbo switch is in the computer's setup program. You must run the setup program to turn Turbo Mode on or off.

Your hard disk is packed with lost pieces of files. If you reset or warm boot your computer in the middle of something, you get bits and pieces of unnamed files saved to your hard disk. This can bog down the disk. To get rid of these pieces, you first have to find them and give them names. Type **chkdsk /f** at the C:> prompt and press **Enter**. DOS saves the pieces in a series of files that end in .CHK. I've never met a .CHK file that was good for anything. You can delete them by typing **del \file*.chk** and pressing **Enter**.

Files are fragmented on your hard disk. When you save files to disk, the parts of the file may be stored on different parts of the disk. Whenever you try to open or use the file, your hard disk has to jump around to find all its parts. To defragment the files, use a utility program, as explained in the next chapter.

When in Doubt, Get the Heck Out

If no fix works, try rebooting your computer by pressing **Ctrl+Alt+Del**. If that doesn't work, turn everything off and leave it off for three minutes. (This lets the computer clear its head.) Turn on your monitor, then turn on your printer, and then turn on the system unit. If this doesn't fix it, call for help.

The Least You Need to Know

If you don't remember all the specifics given in this chapter, don't worry. Chances are, your specific problem isn't covered. The important things to remember are how to trace back a problem to its cause. Here are some reminders:

- Don't panic.

- Look all over the screen for any clues.

- Ask yourself when the problem started. Did you install a new program?

- Isolate the problem. Does it happen in all programs or just this one? Does it happen all the time?

- If you suspect a hardware problem, turn everything off and check the connections. Wiggle the plugs; a loose connection can be as bad or worse than no connection.

- As a last resort, turn your computer off, wait three minutes, and then turn everything back on.

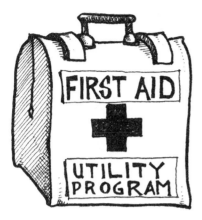

Chapter 21

Zen and the Art of Computer Maintenance

In This Chapter

☛ How to clean your monitor

☛ Getting the crumbs out of your keyboard

☛ How to recover from spilling something on the keyboard

☛ How to clean a mouse

☛ How to dust the printer and system unit

☛ Is it necessary to clean your floppy disk drives?

☛ Why you should keep a utility program on hand

☛ How to prepare against catastrophes and how to recover from them

☛ How to protect your disks and the data that they store

Okay, I admit the chapter title is a little misleading; this chapter doesn't have any Zen in it. Maybe a koan or two—what is the sound of a diskless disk drive? Or a mantra you can chant when you spill Coke all over your keyboard; two words, starts with Oh . . . . But none of the Zen philosophy you'll find in *Zen and the Art of Motorcycle Maintenance*. No, this chapter focuses on the maintenance part.

Not the Car Analogy Again?!

Yes, the car analogy again. Sorry, but it's the perfect analogy, especially when we're talking maintenance. Your computer *is* like a car. You might be able to use it without ever cleaning it, tuning it up, or rotating the tires, but it probably won't last as long or run as well. In this chapter, you will learn some basic computer maintenance that will help keep your computer running trouble free and help you recover from the occasional accident.

You'll learn how to take care of all the parts that make up your computer: getting the crumbs out of your keyboard, cleaning bug juice off your monitor, and sucking the dust out of your system unit. Later in the chapter, you'll learn how to take care of the inside of the computer—the hard disk drive and the data it stores.

Washing the Windshield

If you've never cleaned your monitor, you can probably take your finger and write WASH ME on the screen. Don't wash the monitor yet. Turn it off first. Then take a paper towel, spray some water on the towel, and wipe the dust and fingerprints off the screen. Don't spray anything on the glass part of the monitor. You might get moisture inside the monitor; moisture and electricity don't mix.

> ## By the Way . . .
> For dusting a monitor, try a used dryer sheet. The sheet is soft, so it is less likely to scratch the monitor. And the sheet will help reduce the static on the monitor, preventing future dust build up.

While you're at it, dust the monitor case, but make sure you don't wipe the dust into any of its openings. Having dust *outside* the unit is better than having dust *inside* it. If you have a vacuum cleaner with a hose, use the hose to suck the dust away from the monitor.

Decrumbing the Keyboard

Keyboards are like placemats; anything that falls out of your mouth or off your fingers falls on the keyboard. The keyboard squirrels all this stuff away under the keys. To get it out, turn your keyboard upside down and shake it gently.

> **By the Way . . .**
> More studies on the evils of second hand smoke prove that it harms your computer. The soot can settle on your computer components and disks and cause them to poop out at an early age.

Oops, Coffee on the Keyboard

If you spill coffee, juice, or some other beverage on the keyboard, turn everything off. As long as the moisture doesn't seep deep inside the keyboard, it'll be okay. Dab as much of the fluid off the keys as possible with a paper towel, and then turn the keyboard over. Dry the keyboard with a hair dryer, or allow it to air dry (this may take overnight).

If the keys stick after you dry the keyboard, you may have to take it in for a professional cleaning.

It's best to prevent the spill in the first place. If you must have a mint julep while working, keep your glass below the level of your keyboard, and sit back when you're sipping.

Treating Your Mouse for Fur Balls

You probably feed your mouse without ever knowing it. Your mouse will devour all the dust and crumbs on your desk and get all gummed up inside. This may cause the mouse pointer to start jumping around the screen.

To clean the mouse, turn everything off. Turn the mouse over, unscrew its cap or slide it open, remove the mouse ball, and gently pick any furry looking things out of the mouse with a toothpick or tweezers. There are a few rollers inside the mouse that look like rolls of paper towel. Dust usually collects around these rollers. Also, blow on the contacts inside the mouse to remove dust.

If anything is stuck to the mouse ball, wipe it off with a paper towel dipped in rubbing alcohol. Replace the ball, and screw the cap back on. Good for another 5,000 miles.

Dusting the Printer

Printers commonly get lots of paper dust inside them. Vacuum out the paper dust. There's not much else you can do to keep your printer in top operating condition.

> ### By the Way . . .
> If you have an ink-jet printer, I can tell you one thing not to do. This is a true story. Ink-jet cartridges cost over 15 bucks a shot. I had one that seemingly had run out of ink (it was printing light). I took it out and shook it. I could hear ink sloshing around inside. I figured it must be gummed up, so I took a Q-tip, dipped it in rubbing alcohol, and cleaned all the parts of the cartridge real good. I put it back in, and no print, not a dot. So, I got the manual out. It said you should NEVER NEVER clean the place where the ink squirts out; I cleaned it real good.

Sucking Out the System Unit

Hate to break it to you, but your system unit is a vacuum cleaner. There's a little fan at the back that sucks air, dust, smoke, and any other surrounding debris into your computer. It's important to keep dust and dirt away from this fan. So, vacuum behind your computer, just as you vacuum under and behind your refrigerator. (Did you know you were supposed to vacuum under your refrigerator every month?)

In addition, you (or a knowledgeable service person) should occasionally take the cover off your system unit and vacuum inside. Be sure the vacuum hose does not touch any of the parts inside the system unit. Do this every year or two.

Cleaning the Floppy Disk Drives: Is This Really Necessary?

You can buy a floppy drive cleaning kit at your local neighborhood computer store. You squirt some goop on a special disk, insert it in the drive, and let it spin-wash your drive. It supposedly cleans the read/write heads inside the drive.

I've never cleaned a floppy disk drive, and I've never had a problem. I've never even met anyone who had a problem with a dirty drive. So, unless you stuck a slice of bread in your floppy drive, thinking it was the toaster, don't worry about cleaning it. If the drive stops working, clean it; it's worth a try.

A First-Aid Kit for Your Computer: A Utility Program

No matter how careful you are, you and your computer will eventually get into an accident. It may be human error or machine malfunction, but sometime (usually the worst possible time), something will go wrong. To recover from the occasional mishap, you should keep a first-aid kit handy. In the following sections, you will learn about computer first-aid kits (utility programs) and what they can do for you.

A utility program consists of a set of programs designed to help you manage your files, get information about your computer, diagnose and repair common problems, recover lost or damaged files, and keep your system operating efficiently. Most utility programs offer the following features:

File and directory maintenance   You can move, copy, and delete files and directories on disk. This allows you to keep your disk organized.

File undelete   If you delete a file accidentally, a utility program will help you get the file back.

Virus protection   This feature checks your computer for viruses or for the effects of viruses and lets you know if your system has been infected.

System information   Provides information about your computer, including how much memory it has, how that memory is being used, how fast the hard disk is, the type of monitor that's connected to the computer, the speed of the central processing unit, and more.

Disk fixing   If a disk is unreadable or if a file on disk gets damaged or lost, the utility program will try to help you find and correct the problem.

Disk performance   As you store files on your hard disk, parts of a file may be stored in different locations on the disk. This makes it more difficult for the disk drive to read the file. Utility programs let you reorganize the files on disk so each file is stored in a single location.

File protection   Most utility programs let you protect your files with passwords to prevent unauthorized people from viewing or changing the file.

File backups   Some utility programs come with a backup program that copies the files from your hard disk to a set of floppy disks or to a separate backup drive. If anything happens to your original files, you can use the backups to restore them.

> ## By the Way . . .
>
> The best file and disk fix program on the market is The Norton Utilities. However, if you want anti-virus protection and a backup program, you have to buy them separately. I prefer PC Tools. It comes with anti-virus protection, a backup utility, and a very easy-to-use work screen. And as far as recovering accidentally deleted files and fixing damaged disks, PC Tools has never failed me.

Preventive Medicine

Although you can usually recover from disaster even if you haven't prepared for it, you have a greater chance of recovering if you protect your system. Commit the five-step preventive medicine plan to memory, and use it.

Step 1: Keep Track of Deleted Files

Utility programs typically offer a delete protection feature that prevents deleted files from being completely obliterated. Delete protection usually comes in two forms:

Name tracking   With name tracking, the utility program keeps track of the names of all the files you delete. As long as you haven't saved another file to disk (over the file you deleted), you can get the deleted file back by selecting its name from a list.

Exact copies   As a more reliable form of protection, some utility programs keep a copy of every file you delete in a separate directory on disk. If you accidentally delete a file, you can get the copy. This feature requires more disk space than the name tracking feature.

TECHNO NERD TEACHES

When you delete a file, only the first letter of the file's name is deleted in the *file allocation table* (FAT)—the index of the files on a diskette or hard disk. This tells DOS that it's okay to write another file onto the disk where the deleted file resides. The actual contents of the file remain on the disk until replaced with new data. As long as you don't record any new information on the disk, you can retrieve any files that you've accidentally deleted.

Step 2: Create a Backup Copy of Vital Disk Information

At the beginning of every disk is some vital information, including a File Allocation Table that tells the computer where all the files on the disk are located. If this information gets wiped out, your computer can come to a grinding halt.

Utility programs contain a program (usually called *mirror*) that takes a snapshot of this vital information and stores it in a separate location on disk. If the original information gets damaged (usually by an accidental format), you can use the mirror copy to get it back.

Formatting programs also make it easier to format floppy disks. Instead of having to use DOS command switches to tell DOS what type of disk you are formatting, you simply select the type from a list of options.

Step 3: Format Safely

One of the most common ways users lose data is by accidentally formatting a disk (this is fairly easy to do in DOS). Formatting wipes all the data from the disk. Most utility programs have a separate formatting program that warns you if a disk has already been formatted or if the disk contains data. You can then cancel the operation.

Step 4: Back Up Your Files on a Regular Basis

A backup program takes the files stored on your hard disk, compresses the files (so they take up less disk space), and stores the compressed files on a set of floppy disks or some other backup medium (such as a tape). If anything happens to your original files, you can restore the files using the backups.

Some utility programs come with a backup program; others don't. If you get a utility program that does not come with a backup, purchase a backup program separately. Although you can back up files with DOS, it's not the easiest way to back up your hard disk.

My three favorite backup programs are CP Backup (which comes alone or with PC Tools), Norton Backup, and FastBack Plus. (FastBack Plus is kind of expensive, and the other two work almost as well.)

Step 5: Create an Emergency Disk

If your hard disk gets trashed, you may not even be able to boot your computer in order to fix the hard disk. In such a case, it is useful to have a bootable floppy disk on hand so you can start your computer and perform the necessary fix. A utility program will help you create such a disk. In addition to being bootable, the disk should contain:

Undelete tools   If you accidentally deleted files on your hard disk, you can run the undelete program from the emergency disk to get the files back.

System information   Your computer stores information, including disk drive information, in a battery-operated storage area. If the battery dies, your computer may forget it has a hard disk. The emergency disk should contain the system information so you can remind your computer where everything is.

An unformat program   If you accidentally format your hard disk, you'll need to unformat it. The emergency disk should contain a program that allows you to unformat a disk.

A disk fix program   Most users don't know where to start when their system crashes. A disk fix program can identify the problem and help you figure out what to do.

CPR for Your Computer

When your computer poops out or you delete a bunch of files by accident, you need help. Utility programs can help you recover from disasters and bring your system back to life. What you need to do to recover from a problem depends on the problem. The next few sections describe some common problems and solutions in no particular order.

When Disaster Strikes

What you do immediately after realizing that you accidentally deleted a file, formatted a disk, or suffered some other computer mishap is a major factor in how likely it is that you can recover the file or disk. Here are three good rules to follow after your blunder:

- ☞ **Don't panic.** If you panic, you are likely to do more damage. You're better off doing nothing than making the wrong move. The problem can't get any worse.

- ☞ **Don't turn your computer off.** By turning your computer off and then on, you risk making the problem worse. Whenever you boot the computer, it may write something to the hard disk, replacing something that was already there. If you turned your computer off, reboot it from a floppy disk. This prevents the computer from using the hard disk.

- ☞ **Don't save or copy any files to the hard disk.** By saving or copying files to the hard disk, you risk writing over the contents of any accidentally deleted files. Don't install a utility program at this point either. Run the utility program from a floppy disk or from an emergency disk.

Bringing Files Back from the Grave

If you cannot find a file or group of files, you may have accidentally deleted the files. Then again, you may have merely misplaced them. Before you try to undelete the files, look around in various directories to see if you can find the files. If you still can't find the files, use the DOS Undelete command (as explained in Chapter 20), or use the utility program to get it back.

Unformatting a Disk

If you accidentally format a disk, you can unformat the disk. With DOS, type **unformat** followed by the letter of the disk drive you want to unformat, and press **Enter**. For example, to unformat the disk in drive A, type **unformat a:** and press **Enter**.

With a utility program, you can usually select the Unformat command from a menu. The program will then lead you through the process of unformatting the disk. If you formatted your hard disk drive, you'll need to boot your computer from a floppy disk and then run the Unformat program from a floppy disk. (Whatever you do, don't try to install the Unformat program, or any program, to your hard disk; it will overwrite existing information on the disk.)

Accidentally unformatting a disk is as bad as accidentally formatting a disk. If you unformat a disk when you don't need to, you destroy any information on the disk.

Curing a Sick Disk

Keep in mind that disks store information magnetically. Now, if the surface of the disk gets scratched or smudged, or if it just wears out, information can get lost. The information may be on the disk; it's just that DOS can't find it. A utility program can help revitalize worn or damaged disks, making it possible for DOS to find the information.

Giving Your Hard Disk a Tune-Up

As you save and delete and save files to a disk, files start to get *fragmented*. That is, all the parts of a file may not be in one place. To read or use the file, the hard drive has to scurry about looking for all the parts. This takes time and places added strain on the drive.

To get the drive running more smoothly, you can use a defragmentation program to unfragment the files on the disk. Most utility programs come with such a tool.

TECHNO NERD TEACHES

To revitalize a disk, most utility programs reformat the disk, one section (*sector*) at a time. The program reads information off a sector (if possible), formats the sector, and then writes the information back onto it. If the sector is damaged, the utility program marks the sector as bad, so DOS won't try to write anything there in the future. The program then writes the data from that sector to a different one. Usually, revitalization will get back most of the lost data.

A Cache Can Make Your Drive Live Longer

DOS, Windows, and most utilities programs come with a disk-caching program. A *cache* (pronounced "cash") acts as your computer's valet. It sets aside some space in your computer's memory for often-used information. Whenever the computer needs this information, the cache is there ready to serve. The computer doesn't have to run back and forth to the disk to get information. A cache increases the speed of your computer and reduces wear and tear on the disk drive, making the drive live a longer life.

Most caching programs work automatically. You just have to set up the program to run when you start your computer.

Defending Your Computer Against Viruses

A computer virus is a program that can get into your system, delete files, and destroy the information that your computer needs to function properly. Left untreated, a computer virus can bring your computer to a grinding halt. Now the good news: viruses are rare.

Computer viruses are not airborne diseases that your computer can mysteriously contract. To contract a virus, your computer must be on, and the virus must be introduced to your system through one of its ports or drives. Your computer may be at risk for catching a virus if:

You are connected to other computers via modem. Your computer is more at risk if you obtain programs from BBS (Bulletin Board System) services or on-line information services and then run the programs.

You are connected to other computers on a network. You can't do much to protect your individual computer in this case. Protection is up to the Network Administrator.

Somebody else uses your computer. If somebody else uses an infected floppy disk on your system, your computer may become infected.

You obtain program or data disks from outside sources. If you use only commercial programs, and you work with only the files you create, your system is safe. If you get disks and programs from user groups, BBSs, or other outside groups, you are more at risk.

Keeping Viruses at Bay

The best way to stop viruses from destroying files is to prevent them from infecting your system. Take a few precautions:

Isolate your system. Don't let anyone insert a floppy disk into your computer without your knowledge. Any disk could contain a virus. If you're hooked up to a modem or if your computer is networked, this type of prevention is not very practical or effective.

Write-protect program disks. Before you install a commercial program, write-protect the disks you purchased. If your hard disk is infected with a virus, the write-protection will at least protect the program disks. You can then use the disks to reinstall the program after you destroy the virus.

Back up your data files separately. Although viruses can wipe out data files, viruses rarely infect them.

Install an anti-virus program. Anti-virus programs prevent viruses from infecting your system and warn you of incoming viruses. Some popular anti-virus programs for the IBM include FluShot+, Norton AntiVirus, and Central Point's Anti-Virus.

The Least You Need to Know

Computer maintenance may seem like a lot of busy work at first, but once you establish good computing habits, you will hardly miss the little time it takes. Here are the ten most important maintenance tasks you should perform:

☞ Clean the dust off your monitor, so you can see what you're doing.

continues

continued

☛ If you spill something on your keyboard, turn everything off and dry the keyboard.

☛ If your mouse pointer is getting jumpy, turn everything off and clean your mouse.

☛ Don't worry about cleaning your floppy disk drives.

☛ Get a utility program and learn how to use it.

☛ Run a mirror program on your hard disk daily. You can usually set the program up to run first thing in the morning.

☛ Back up the files on your disks. Each month, back up the entire disk. Each day, back up the files that have changed that day.

☛ Create an emergency disk for recovering from inevitable accidents, and keep the disk up-to-date.

☛ Run a defragmentation program on your computer at least once every month.

☛ Don't use any disks or files from any questionable sources.

Part Four

Other Stuff You May or May Not Want to Know

This section contains some information I wanted to put in the book but couldn't decide where to put. (I hate to leave anything out.) What sorts of information? Information about some programs I like, how much they cost, and what you should actually pay for them. I even tell you where to get programs at reduced prices.

You also get a list of all the terms I defined in the book (and some that I didn't define), complete with definitions for each term. You can use this list of definitions as a miniglossary to help you translate the language of computer geeks, or to learn how to speak like a geek yourself. (I know, at this very moment, you are whispering to yourself, "Oh boy!")

Chapter 22

Programs I'd Buy If You Gave Me the Money

In This Chapter

- ☛ Software you should consider getting for your new computer
- ☛ Why you should use Microsoft Windows
- ☛ Why you should use a mouse
- ☛ My personal picks of the best program in each software category
- ☛ Some popular programs for home use
- ☛ Why you should never pay the suggested retail price for a program
- ☛ Getting programs for less through mail-order companies
- ☛ How to comparison shop without getting ripped off

Before we begin, let me warn you that this chapter contains *my* recommendations about the kinds of software you should get for your computer, and I'm fairly opinionated. I'm going to tell you exactly how to set up your computer for the end of the 20th Century. I'm going to assume you have at least a 386 20MHz computer with an 80 megabyte hard disk and that you want to be able to harness its power.

Of course, I understand that you may have to settle for less. Computers are money pits, and you can't afford to buy everything. But at least consider my recommendations, and if you have a few extra grand lying around, try out some of my suggestions. You won't be disappointed.

Microsoft Windows: Anything Else Is Neanderthal

Many people are still playing around in DOS. They like their old programs, their old command system, their old way of doing things. Hey, change is hard.

However, assuming you have a relatively speedy computer, and assuming you don't have an old program and an old way of doing things that you need to forget, get Windows. Microsoft Windows, and the programs written for Windows, offer the best technology on the market.

Get Microsoft Windows 3.1, Not 3.0

Microsoft Windows 3.1 comes with some advanced features and improvements over Windows 3.0. The biggest improvement for most folks is that Windows 3.1 offers TrueType fonts. These fonts give you more control over the size and style of your type, no matter what kind of printer you have.

Asking price: $149

Street price: $89 (Microsoft Windows comes free with many new computers.)

Get a Mouse

In order to use Microsoft Windows without going bonkers, get a mouse or trackball. How much should you pay? That depends on what you want:

Bona fide Microsoft mouse: $80-$90

Middle-of-the-road mouse: $50-$60

El cheapo mouse: $25-$30

Trackball: $75-$150

Build the Rest of Your System Around Windows

Most programs come in two versions: DOS and Windows. Many people get Microsoft Windows, and then they use it to run only DOS programs. What's the point? If you have Windows, purchase Windows-compatible programs.

If the program does not have a Windows version, ask the salesperson if a Windows version is due to come out. If the salesperson waffles and says, "Gee, I don't know," call the manufacturer and ask. Most software companies have a Windows version of every program, or they're working on it.

Integrated Software: A Good Place to Start

If you don't really know what you want to do yet, get an integrated program (see Chapter 17). The best beginning level program for Windows is Microsoft Works for Windows.

Microsoft Works for Windows

Asking price: $199

Street price: $129

If you want a more advanced integrated program, try Microsoft Office or SmartSuite. Both of these programs are actually bundles of stand-alone programs. SmartSuite (from Lotus) comes with Lotus 1-2-3 for Windows, Ami Pro (an excellent word-processing program), Freelance Graphics (a business graphics program), and cc:Mail (an E-mail program). Microsoft office comes with Excel, Microsoft Word, PowerPoint (a business graphics program), and Microsoft Mail. Both have a street price of about $450. Ouch!

A Database? What Kind?

The database you should get depends on what you want to do and how you like to work. For example, I'm very disorganized. I have a stack of Post-It notes that I use to keep track of everything from doctor appointments to color settings for my monitor. So I like using the following free-form database, because it works like I do.

Info Select

Asking Price: $149

Street Price: NA

If you need something more structured, try FileMaker Pro from Claris:

FileMaker Pro

Asking Price: $399

Street Price: $269

Desktop Publishing: Fancy or Easy?

If you want a desktop publishing program that's quick and easy to learn and use, get the Microsoft product. I have used several desktop publishing programs, and Microsoft Publisher is the one I keep coming back to for my daily needs. Even my six-year-old son can create great-looking greeting cards and other publications with Publisher.

Microsoft Publisher

Asking Price: $199

Street Price: $129

For a more powerful desktop publishing program, try Aldus PageMaker:

PageMaker

Asking Price: $795

Street Price: $489

Business Presentation Graphics: There's Only One Choice

In the business presentation graphics arena are two programs that stand above the rest: Harvard Graphics and Microsoft PowerPoint. I prefer PowerPoint, because it is designed for Windows. Harvard Graphics has all sorts of weird ways of doing things (they just couldn't get used to Windows).

Microsoft PowerPoint for Windows

Asking Price: $495

Street Price: $315

CorelDRAW! for Graphics

Microsoft Windows comes with a paint program (Microsoft Paintbrush). Microsoft Works for Windows comes with a drawing program. If you want something more advanced, get CorelDRAW!. CorelDRAW! is easy to learn and use and is a powerful tool for creating full-color advertisements.

CorelDRAW!

Asking Price: $595

Street Price: $389

Telecommunications: Not Much of a Choice

Windows comes with a simple telecommunications program. If you want a more advanced program, one that can automate your phone calls, get PROCOMM PLUS. Nothing else comes close.

PROCOMM PLUS for Windows

Asking Price: $149

Street Price: $95

Spreadsheets: Excel or Quattro Pro?

In DOS, Lotus is the king of spreadsheets. In Windows, two programs fight for the top spot: Microsoft Excel and Quattro Pro for Windows. I prefer Quattro Pro.

Quattro Pro for Windows

Asking Price: $495

Street Price: $309

> ### By the Way . . .
> Of course, if all you need to do is average a column or row of numbers, or perform other minor calculations, you can use a less expensive spreadsheet. Excel and Quattro Pro are industrial strength.

Utilities: More for Your Buck with PC Tools

Norton Utilities is still top dog when it comes to data recovery. However, for the average Joe, PC Tools gives you an easier (though slightly less reliable) way of recovering data. For the same price, PC Tools offers additional features, including virus detection and elimination, file backup and restore, an advanced DOS Shell, memory management, and a completely integrated program.

PC Tools

Asking Price: $179

Street Price: $129

Word Processors: Microsoft Wins Again

The most popular word processing program is WordPerfect for DOS. In the Windows arena, WordPerfect can still hold its own, but many users find it too DOSsy for Windows. The two top contenders in this category are Ami Pro and Microsoft Word 2.0 for Windows. And again, the Microsoft product wins out, but not by much.

Microsoft Word 2.0 for Windows

Asking Price: $495

Street Price: $299

Popular Software for the Home

In addition to the business giants listed above, you can get software to help you around the house. Following is a list of some popular programs for the home. The price listed is the asking price. You can usually get the programs for a lot less.

Typing Tutor 5 ($49.95)　Typing Tutor tests your typing ability and designs lessons for your skill level. The program takes note of the keys you are having trouble with and drills you on those keys. In addition, the program contains a game called Letter Invaders to help you practice typing while you play.

The New Print Shop ($59.95)   The New Print Shop is an ideal program for novice desktop publishers. With Print Shop, you can design and print your own greeting cards, invitations, announcements, and stationery, and customize each publication. I'm not all that sold on this product, but lots of people like it.

OnTime for Windows ($129.95)   With OnTime, you can create and print calendars for a week, month, or year; make appointments to include on the calendar; have the computer remind you of upcoming appointments; and keep track of birthdays, anniversaries, and other important occasions.

Home Medical Advisor ($69.95)   Home Medical Advisor offers a complete medical library containing the following volumes: Symptoms, Diseases, Injury, Poisons, Tests, Rx Drugs, and Referrals. You select the volume and select a topic from the volume to quickly find the information you need.

TurboTax for Windows ($99.95)   TurboTax does your taxes for you. You enter information about your income and deductions, and TurboTax completes and prints all the necessary forms. TurboTax also provides you with suggestions for saving money and can perform a preliminary tax audit to warn you of missing information or risky entries.

Quicken 2 for Windows ($69.95)   Quicken is a personal finance program that lets you write and print checks, automatically balances your checkbook, and helps you keep a balanced budget. Although commonly used for home finances, the program is also good for managing a small business.

AutoMap for Windows ($99.95)   AutoMap gives you a map of the United States, complete with the highway system. You specify a departure point and a destination, and AutoMap determines the fastest and the shortest routes. If you don't like to take the interstates, tell AutoMap, and it will reroute you using only back roads. Includes information about parks and landmarks as well.

Never Pay the Suggested Retail Price

The first lesson in computer shopping is "Don't pay the suggested retail price, and beware of buying directly from the manufacturer." Software and hardware manufacturers commonly set a high suggested retail price for their product so dealers can offer great bargains. You can usually get a program for 1/3 to 1/2 off the suggested retail price by buying it through a mail-order company or through a discount software store, such as Egghead Software or Software etc.

By the Way . . .

If you don't know of any mail-order companies, buy a magazine such as *PC Computing* and call one of the mail-order companies that has an ad in the magazine. They will be more than happy to send you a catalog. I got my street prices from a place called MicroWarehouse (1-800-367-7080). For an extra seven bucks, you can get your toys delivered the next day.

Before You Buy

When shopping for a program, don't compare just prices. Some clearing houses will try to sell you a previous version of a program real cheap. Find out the version number of the most recent version of the program. Then shop around for the best price for that version.

The Least You Need to Know

When shopping for a software package, you have a lot to keep in mind. However, if you go the Windows route, you narrow the field quite a bit. So, here's a rundown of what I would do if I were you:

- ☞ Ditch DOS, get Microsoft Windows, and build your system around it. Make sure you get Windows 3.1.

- ☞ No, I don't work for Microsoft Corporation.

- ☞ Get a mouse. Working in Windows without a mouse is like eating chicken with a fork.

- ☞ If you don't know where to start, get an integrated program, which will provide a spreadsheet, database, and word processor.

- ☞ Most Microsoft products run well under Windows, but Microsoft does not always have the best product in a given category.

- ☞ Info Select is a good database for storing random pieces of information.

- ☞ For desktop publishing, Microsoft Publisher is a good program for creating newsletters, brochures, greeting cards, and other short publications.

- ☞ In the utilities arena, PC Tools offers more features for less money than any program on the market.

- ☞ If you are looking for a powerful word processing program, try WordPerfect for DOS or Microsoft Word 2.0 for Windows.

- ☞ Never pay the suggested retail price.

- ☞ When purchasing a program, make sure you get the latest version.

Speak Like a Geek: The Complete Archive

The computer world is like a big exclusive club complete with its own language. If you want to be accepted, you need to learn the lingo. The following miniglossary will help you get started.

access time   The average time it takes a device (usually a disk drive) to find a random piece of data on a disk. Access time is measured in milliseconds (the lower the number, the faster the drive). Good access times are between 15 ms and 20 ms. (See also *transfer rate*.)

application   Also known as *program*, a set of instructions that enables a computer to perform a specific task, such as word processing or data management.

ASCII file   A file containing characters that can be used by any program on any computer. Sometimes called a *text file* or an *ASCII text file*. (ASCII is pronounced "ask-key.")

AUTOEXEC.BAT   A file that DOS reads whenever you boot or reboot your computer. This file contains a series of commands that DOS automatically reads and executes.

batch file   Any file that contains a series of commands. You run the batch file, just as you would run a program file (by entering its name at the DOS prompt). The most famous batch file is AUTOEXEC.BAT.

baud   A unit for measuring the speed of data transmission, usually used to describe the speed at which a modem transfers data, such as 2400 baud. A more accurate measure of transmission speed is bps (bits per second).

BIOS (basic input-output system)   The start-up instructions for a computer. The BIOS tells the computer how to control traffic between the various elements that make up the computer, including disk drives, the printer, the ports, and the monitor.

bit-mapped graphics   With a paint program, your image is stored as a map of the pixels which make up the image. The map contains a collection of bits; each bit specifies the location and color of one pixel. Hence, the objects are referred to as *bit-mapped graphics*.

boot   To start a computer with the operating system software (usually DOS) in place.

buffer   A temporary storage area. A buffer usually stands between two devices and feeds data from one device to another. A print buffer is often used to store data in memory or on disk until the printer is ready for it. This allows the fast talking computer to talk slow enough for the printer to understand.

bulletin board system (BBS)   A program that enables a computer to automatically answer the phone when other computers call. The BBS allows the calling computer to copy files to it (*upload* files) and copy files from it (*download* files). Although you can purchase a BBS program to set up your own BBS, most users work with BBS's set up by computer companies and professional associations.

bus   A superhighway that carries information electronically from one part of the computer to another. There are three such highways:

- *Data bus*. Lets data travel back and forth between memory and the microprocessor.

- *Address bus*. Carries information about the locations (addresses) of specific information.

- *Control bus*. Carries control signals to make sure traffic flows smoothly, without confusion.

bus architecture   The infrastructure of a computer that determines how much information the processor can process at one time: 8 bits, 16 bits, or 32 bits. Think of it as lanes on a highway; a 32-lane highway can handle more traffic than can an 8-lane highway.

byte   A group of eight bits that usually represents a character or a digit. For example, the byte 01000001 represents the letter A.

cache   Pronounced "cash," this is a part of memory that makes your computer run faster by holding the most recently accessed data from a disk. The next time the computer needs the data, the computer gets it from memory rather than from the disk, which would be slower. Sometimes called a *RAM cache*.

capacity   A measure of how much data a disk can store. For example, a 5 1/4-inch, high-density floppy disk can be formatted to store 1.2MB; 1.2MB is the disk's *capacity*.

CD-ROM (compact-disk read-only memory)   A storage technology that uses the same kind of disks you play in an audio CD player for mass storage of computer data. A single disk can store over 600MB of information. Pronounced "see-dee-rahm."

cell   The box formed by the intersection of a row (1,2,3...) and column (A,B,C...) in a spreadsheet. Each cell has an *address* (such as B12) that defines its column and row. A cell may contain text, a numeric value, or a formula.

click   To move the mouse pointer over an object or icon and press and release the mouse button once without moving the mouse.

clipboard   A temporary storage area that holds text and graphics. The cut and copy commands put text or graphics on the clipboard, erasing the clipboard's previous contents. The paste command copies clipboard data to a document.

clone   A derogatory term used to describe a compatible computer assembled by a local computer dealer. Clone computers have the same status as generic food—they cost less, but may not offer the same quality as the name-brand compatibles. I say *may not* because some clones are actually superior to their name-brand counterparts.

CMOS (Complementary Metal-Oxide Semiconductor)   Pronounced "SEA-moss," CMOS is an electronic device (usually battery operated) that stores information about your computer. Information stored in CMOS includes the current date and time (if your computer is equipped with a clock) and the number and type of disk drives your computer has. If the information in CMOS is damaged by battery failure or a system glitch, you may not be able to use the hard drive, and information may mysteriously disappear from your disk. Some utility programs, such as PC Tools, provide a way to restore the lost or damaged CMOS information and allow you to test the CMOS battery.

COM port   Short for COMmunications port. A receptacle, usually at the back of the computer, into which you can plug a serial device, such as a modem, mouse, or serial printer. COM ports are numbered COM1, COM2, and so on.

command   An order that tells the computer what to do. In command-driven programs, you have to press a specific key or type the command to execute it. With menu-driven programs, you select the command from a menu.

communications software   A set of instructions that allows a computer (equipped with the necessary hardware, such as a modem) to communicate with other computers through the telephone lines.

computer   Any machine that accepts input (from a user), processes the input, and produces output in some form.

CPU (Central Processing Unit)   See *microprocessor*.

crash   Failure of a system or program. Usually, you realize that your system has crashed when the display or keyboard locks up. The term *crash* is also used to refer to a disk crash or head crash. A disk crash occurs when the read/write head in the disk drive falls on the disk. This would be like dropping a phonograph needle on a record. A disk crash can destroy any data stored where the read/write head fell on the disk.

cursor   A horizontal line that appears below characters. A cursor acts like the tip of your pencil; anything you type appears at the cursor. (See also *insertion point*.)

data   Technically speaking, the facts and figures that you enter into the computer and that are stored and used by the computer. When data is put into some meaningful form, such as a document or report, it is called *information*. In short, you enter data, and the computer gives you information. In common usage, *data* and *information* are used interchangeably.

database   A type of computer program used for storing, organizing, and retrieving information. Popular database programs include dBASE, Paradox, and Q&A.

default mode   The initial settings that are in place when you start a program or begin creating a file. With defaults, the computer essentially tells you, "If you don't choose an option, I'll choose one for you."

density   A measure of the amount of data that can be stored per square inch of storage area on a disk. To understand density, think of a disk covered with magnetic dust. Each particle of dust stores one piece of data. No matter how large or small the particle, it still stores only one piece of data. With double-density disks, the particles are large, so the disk can hold fewer particles (less data). With high-density disks, the particles are small, so more particles can be packed in less space, and the disk can store more data.

desktop publishing (DTP)   A program that allows you to combine text and graphics on the same page and manipulate the text and graphics on-screen. Desktop publishing programs are commonly used to create newsletters, brochures, flyers, resumes, and business cards.

dialog box   In many programs, you can enter a simple command to perform some task, such as saving a file. However, you may need to enter additional information before the program can perform the task. In such cases, the program may display a dialog box, which allows you to carry on a "conversation" with the program.

dictionaries   Many programs offer *dictionaries* and boast the number of words included. Don't expect these dictionaries to function as Webster's Ninth. The dictionaries are used by the spell-checking feature to determine correct spellings; most of these dictionaries don't contain definitions.

directory   Because large hard disks can store thousands of files, you often need to store related files in separate directories on the disk. Think of your disk as a filing cabinet and think of each directory as a drawer in the filing cabinet. By keeping files in separate directories, it is easier to locate and work with related files.

disk   A round, flat, magnetic storage medium. See *floppy disk* and *hard disk*.

disk drive   A device that writes data to a magnetic disk and reads data from the disk. Think of a disk drive as a cassette recorder/player. Just as the cassette player can record sounds on a magnetic cassette tape and play back those sounds, a disk drive can record data on a magnetic disk and play back that data.

document   Any work you create using an application program and that you save in a file on disk. Although the term *document* traditionally refers to work created in a word-processing program, such as a letter or a chapter of a book, *document* is now loosely used to refer to any work, including spreadsheets and databases.

DOS (disk operating system)   DOS, which rhymes with "boss," is an essential program that provides the necessary instructions for the computer's parts (keyboard, disk drive, central processing unit, display screen, printer, and so on) to function as a unit.

DOS prompt   An on-screen prompt that indicates DOS is ready to accept a command. It looks something like **C>** or **C:**.

download   To copy files from another computer to your computer usually through a modem. See also *upload*.

E-mail   Short for *electronic mail*, E-mail is a system that lets people send and receive messages from computer to computer. E-mail is usually available on networks and on-line information services.

EMS (Expanded Memory Specification)   See *expanded memory*.

environment   An *environment* is a setting in which you perform tasks on your computer. Microsoft Windows, for example, displays a graphical environment that lets you enter commands by selecting pictures rather than by typing commands. This makes it much easier to use your computer (assuming you know what the pictures stand for).

executable file   A program file that can run the program. Executable files end in .BAT, .COM, or .EXE.

expanded memory   A special way for IBM computers to use memory beyond 640 kilobytes. With expanded memory, additional memory is added to the computer in the form of memory chips or a memory board. To access this additional memory, an expanded memory manager reserves 64 of the standard 640 kilobytes of memory as a swap area. The 64 kilobytes represent 4 *pages,* each page consisting of 16 kilobytes. Pages of data are swapped into and out of this 64 kilobyte region from expanded memory at a high speed. Not all programs can use expanded memory. See also, *extended memory*.

expansion slot   When you purchase a computer, it usually comes equipped with several ports (receptacles) into which you can plug peripheral equipment (such as a printer, modem, and mouse). With many computers, you can add ports for plugging in additional peripherals, such as scanners and sound boards. The port is connected to a circuit board that you can plug into a receptacle inside your computer. The place where you plug the board in is called an *expansion slot*.

extended memory   Extended memory is the same sort of memory that makes up the one megabyte of base memory that most PCs have. Extended memory is directly available to the processor in your computer, unlike expanded memory in which data must be swapped into and out of the base memory. Because of this, extended memory is faster than expanded memory. If needed, you can customize a portion of extended memory to act like expanded memory for use with programs that can use only expanded memory. See also *expanded memory*.

extension   In DOS, each file you create has a unique name. The name consists of two parts: a file name and an extension. The file name can be up to eight characters. The extension (which is optional) can be up to three characters.

field   In a database record, a field contains a single piece of information (for example, a telephone number, ZIP code, or a person's last name).

file   A collection of information stored as a single unit on a floppy or hard disk. Files always have a file name to identify them.

file allocation table (FAT)   A map on every disk that tells the operating system where the files on the disk are stored. It's sort of like a classroom seating chart.

fixed disk drive   A disk drive that has a non-removable disk, as opposed to floppy drives, in which you can insert and remove disks.

floppy disk   A wafer encased in plastic that magnetically stores data (the facts and figures you enter and save). Floppy disks are the disks you insert in your computer's floppy disk drive (located on the front of the computer).

font   Any set of characters of the same *typeface* (design) and *type size* (measured in points). For example, Times Roman 12-point is a font; Times Roman is the typeface, and 12-point is the size. (There are 72 points in an inch.)

format (disk)   Formatting creates a map on the disk that tells the operating system how the disk is structured. The operating system uses this map to keep track of where files are stored.

format (document)   To establish the physical layout of a document, including page size, margins, running heads, line spacing, text alignment, graphics placement, and so on.

function keys   The 10 or 12 F keys on the left side of the keyboard or 12 F keys at the top of the keyboard. F keys are numbered F1, F2, F3, and so on. These keys are used to enter various commands in a program.

graphical user interface (GUI, pronounced "gooey")   A type of program interface that uses graphical elements, such as icons, to represent commands, files, and (in some cases) other programs. The most famous GUI is Microsoft Windows.

hard disk   A disk drive that comes complete with a non-removable disk. It acts as a giant floppy disk drive and usually sits inside your computer.

Hayes-compatible   Used to describe a modem that uses the Hayes command set for communicating with other modems over the phone lines. Hayes-compatible modems usually are preferred over other modems because they are more standard.

icon   A graphic image that represents another object, such as a file on a disk.

income and expense categories   Personal finance programs use *income* and *expense categories* to keep track of money coming in and going out. For example, you may have expense categories for salary, clothing, and auto. When you generate a budget report, the program adds all the numbers in the category and gives you the totals.

initialize   To reset a computer or program to some starting values. When used to describe floppy or hard disks, the term means the same as format.

insertion point   A blinking vertical line used in some word processors to indicate the place where any characters you type will be inserted. An insertion point is the equivalent of a *cursor*.

integrated program   A program that combines the features of several programs, such as a word processor, spreadsheet, database, and communications program. The names of integrated programs usually end with the word *Works*.

interface   A link between two objects, such as a computer and a modem. The link between a computer and a person is called a *user interface*, and refers to the way a person communicates with the computer.

keyboard   The main input device for most computers.

kilobyte (K)   A unit for measuring the amount of data. A kilobyte is equivalent to 1,024 bytes.

load   To read data or program instructions from disk and place them in the computer's memory, where the computer can use the data or instructions. You usually load a program before you use it or load a file before you edit it.

logical drive   A section of a hard disk or memory that is treated as a separate disk and is assigned its own letter. For example, you may *partition* your hard drive into logical drives C, D, E, and F. It's still one disk, but it is partitioned into logical drives.

macro   A recorded set of instructions for a frequently used task that can be activated by pressing a specified key combination. Macros resemble small programs.

megabyte   A standard unit used to measure the storage capacity of a disk and the amount of computer memory. A megabyte is 1,048,576 bytes (1,000 kilobytes). This is roughly equivalent to 500 pages of double-spaced text. Megabyte is commonly abbreviated as M, MB, or Mbyte.

memory An electronic storage area inside the computer, used to temporarily store data or program instructions when the computer is using them. The computer's memory is erased when the power to the computer is turned off.

menu A list of commands or instructions displayed on the screen. Menus organize commands and make a program easier to use.

microprocessor Sometimes called the Central Processing Unit (CPU) or processor, this chip is the computer's brain; it does all the calculations for the computer.

modem An acronym for MOdulator/DEModulator. A modem lets a computer send and receive data through an ordinary telephone line.

monitor A television-like screen that lets the computer display information.

mouse A handheld device that you move across the desktop to move an indicator, called a mouse pointer, across the screen. Used instead of the keyboard to select and move items (such as text or graphics), execute commands, and perform other tasks.

MS-DOS (Microsoft Disk Operating System) See *DOS*.

multitasking The ability to run two programs at the same time. Some programs, such as the DOS Shell, allow you to switch between two or more programs (task-switching), but do not allow a program to perform operations in the background (multitasking).

object-oriented graphics Draw programs are often called *object-oriented* graphics programs, because they treat objects as individual units rather than as a collection of pixels.

on-line Connected, turned on, and ready to accept information. Used most often in reference to a printer or modem.

palette   A selection of styles and colors available in graphics programs, just like an artist's palette.

parallel port   A connector used to plug a device, usually a printer, into the computer. Transferring data through a parallel port is much faster than transferring data through a serial port, but parallel cables cannot reliably carry data very far.

partition   A hard disk drive can be divided (or *partitioned*) into one or more drives, which DOS refers to as drive C, drive D, drive E, and so on. (Don't be fooled; it's still one disk drive.) The actual hard disk drive is called the *physical* drive; each partition is called a *logical* drive.

path   The route that the computer travels from the root directory to any subdirectories when locating a file.

peripheral   The system unit is the central part of the computer. Any devices that are attached to the system unit are considered *peripheral* (as in "peripheral vision"). Peripheral devices include the monitor, printer, keyboard, mouse, modem, and joystick. Some manufacturers consider the keyboard and monitor as essential parts of the computer rather than as peripherals.

personal finance program   Personal finance programs are often called *check-writing* programs, because their main purpose is to help you keep a balanced checkbook. However, these programs are becoming more diverse. Some personal finance programs can be used to manage the finances of a small business, and others (such as WealthStarter) contain tools for teaching you how to invest your money intelligently.

pixel   A dot of light that appears on the computer screen. A collection of pixels forms characters and images on the screen. Think of a pixel as a single peg in a Lite Brite toy.

ports   The receptacles at the back of the computer. They get their name from the ports where ships pick up and deliver cargo. In this case, the ports allow information to enter and leave the system unit.

POST (Power-On Self Test)   A series of internal checks the computer performs on itself whenever it is first turned on. If the test reveals that any component is not working properly, the computer displays an error message on-screen giving a general indication of which component is causing problems.

program   A group of instructions which tells the computer what to do. Typical programs are word processors, spreadsheets, databases, and games.

prompt   A computer's way of asking for more information. The computer basically looks at you and says, "Tell me something." In other words, the computer is *prompting* you or *prodding* you for information or for a command.

protocol   A group of communications settings that control the transfer of data between two computers via modem.

pull-down menu   A menu that appears at the top of the screen, listing various options. The menu is not visible until you select it from the menu bar. The menu then drops down, covering a small part of the screen.

random-access memory (RAM)   What your computer uses to temporarily store data and programs. RAM is measured in kilobytes and megabytes. Generally if a computer has more RAM, it can run more powerful programs.

record   Used by databases to denote a unit of related information contained in one or more fields, such as an individual's name, address, and phone number.

ROM BIOS   See *BIOS*.

scanner   A device that converts images, such as photographs or printed text, into an electronic format that a computer can use. Many stores use a special type of scanner to read bar code labels into the cash register.

scroll   To move text up and down or right and left on a computer screen.

shell   A program that lets you enter operating system commands by choosing from a menu. Shell programs make the operating system easier to use.

slide   Some presentation programs refer to each "page" in a presentation as a *chart*. Other programs call each "page" a *slide* and refer to the presentation as a *slide show*.

software   Any instructions that tell your computer (the hardware) what to do. There are two types of software: operating system software and application software. *Operating system software* (such as DOS) gets your computer up and running. *Application software* allows you to do something useful, such as type a letter or chase lemmings.

spreadsheet   A program used for keeping schedules and calculating numeric results. Common spreadsheets include Lotus 1-2-3, Microsoft Excel, and Quattro Pro.

style   A collection of specifications for formatting text. A style may include information for the font, size, style, margins, and spacing. Applying a style to text automatically formats the text according to the style's specifications.

switch   A value you can add to a command to control the manner in which the command is carried out. For example, in DOS, you can use the /V switch with the COPY command to have DOS verify that the copied files are exact duplicates of the originals.

trackball   A device that works like an upside-down mouse and requires less desk space for use. Instead of moving the mouse around the desk to move the pointer on-screen, a trackball lets you roll a ball in place to move the pointer. Some arcade video games use devices similar to track balls.

transfer rate   A measure of how much information a device (usually a disk drive) can transfer from the disk to your computer's memory in a second. A good transfer rate is in the range of 500 to 600 kilobytes per second. The higher the number, the faster the drive. (See also *access time*.)

uninterruptible power supply (UPS)   A battery-powered device that protects against power spikes and power outages. If the power goes out, the UPS continues supplying power to the computer so you can continue working or safely turn off your computer without losing any data.

upload   To send data to another computer, usually through a modem and a telephone line or through a network connection.

virus   A program that attaches itself to other files on a floppy or hard disk and duplicates itself without the user's knowledge. The virus attacks the computer by erasing files from the hard disk or by formatting the disk.

widow/orphan   A *widow* is the last line of a paragraph that appears alone at the top of the next page. If the first line of the paragraph gets stranded at the bottom of a page, it is called an *orphan*. Just remember that an orphan is left behind.

wild card   Any character that takes the place of another character or a group of characters. Think of a wild-card character as a wild card in a game of poker. If the Joker is wild, you can use it in place of any card in the entire deck of cards. In DOS, you can use two wild characters: a question mark (?) and an asterisk (*). The question mark stands in for a single character. The asterisk stands in for a group of characters.

windows   A way of displaying information in different parts of the screen. Often used as a nickname for Microsoft Windows.

word processor   A program that lets you enter, edit, format, and print text.

word wrap A feature that automatically moves a word to the next line if the word won't fit at the end of the current line.

write-protect To prevent a computer from adding or modifying data stored on a disk.

Index

delete - go to dosshell
click program
click file
delete

windows file manager
INS key